AS THE TOWERS FELL

AS THE TOWERS FELL

STORIES OF UNSHAKABLE FAITH ON 9/11

LISA CHILSON-ROSE

new
hope
PUBLISHERS

Birmingham, Alabama

New Hope® Publishers
P. O. Box 12065
Birmingham, AL 35202-2065
www.newhopepubl.com

Library of Congress Cataloging-in-Publication Data
Chilson-Rose, Lisa.
As the towers fell : stories of unshakable faith on 9-11 / by Lisa
Chilson-Rose.
p. cm.
ISBN 1-56309-760-5 (pbk.)
1. Christian biography-United States. 2. September 11 Terrorist
Attacks, 2001—Religious aspects-Christianity. I. Title.
BR1700.3.C48 2003
277.47'1083—dc21
2003009261

ISBN: 1-56309-760-5

N034118 • 0803 • 8.5M1

This book is dedicated to all those in the metro New York area who felt and still feel the effects of 9-11-01. May God get all the glory for the good things He has done in the midst of a senseless act of cowardice.

A percentage of the proceeds will go to further the ministry and outreach of Fellowship of Christian Firefighters/ Metro New York and Cops for Christ/ Metro New York.

TABLE OF CONTENTS

Section 3: Faithful to Carry On

And Now . . . My Story

ACKNOWLEDGMENTS

September 11, 2001, changed our lives in the metro New York area in ways that are too numerous to list. These past two years have been tumultuous to say the least, but despite it all, we have come through it. The folks in this book, both those who died and those who survived, will show you how God can work in the most difficult of circumstances. As Christians, we are told in the Bible that hard times will come. There is a verse in the Book of Revelation that says, "Do not fear any of those things which you are about to suffer. . . . Be faithful until death, and I will give you the crown of life" (Revelation 2:10 NKJV). You will read about Christians who were faithful to the end, those who stayed faithful through the hard years after 9-11, and those who came to a faith that will be with them eternally. You will meet ordinary people who lived or live extraordinary lives. May you be inspired by their lives and their intimate relationship with the Creator God and His Son, Jesus Christ. Going through this arduous time has proven them faithful in their relationship and in living for what they know is the truth.

Without the relationship I have with the Lord Jesus Christ, the inspiration of this book would not have happened. What started out as an idea turned into a calling. I thank God for entrusting me with this opportunity.

Without the kindness and patience of my husband Russ, who cooked many a meal, edited chapters, washed clothes, and gave up time alone with his new bride, this book would have never happened. I love you, honey!

Without the encouragement and "cheerleading" of my very good friend and coworker, Michael Chance, I would have probably given up. Michael, you're the best!

Without the perseverance of my assistant, Jill Pittman, in transcribing the interviews, I would still be typing this book! Thanks, Jill. You're a testimony of servanthood to me.

Without the love, support, and prayers of family and friends far and near and my co-workers in the Metropolitan New York Baptist Association, this experience would not have been as fun and challenging and adventurous as it has been. I love you all more than you know! Thanks for believing in me.

And last but certainly not least, I thank the people who shared their stories, or the story of a loved one, for this book. Every person shared with the intent of glorifying the Father in heaven, whom they love. They were telling a story that needed to be told! Thanks for entrusting me with your hearts. May you see His continued healing and strength in your lives every day!

FAITHFUL UNTO DEATH

1

ALFRED J. BRACA

Praying as the Towers Fell

On September 11, 2001, Al Braca began his work-day at his office on the 104th floor of One World Trade Center. He had been a vice presi-dent/ bond broker for Cantor Fitzgerald for 16 years. He was on the phone that morning when an earsplitting explosion happened beneath him. The person on the phone with Al heard people yelling "Evacuate!" in the background; then the phones went dead. Those were the last words spoken by Al Braca to anyone outside the building.

The plane had hit several floors below, at about the 90th floor. Cantor Fitzgerald offices were above the crash site; most likely people in Al's office were trapped. Many people, as the nation saw in news reports, were trying to get to the roof via the windows and ledges because the heat and smoke were penetrating the upper floors rapidly. They did not make it. Al and his colleagues were probably trapped and couldn't go down to get out. Al's wife, Jeannie, knew by the end of the day that her hus-band had died. Al was the kind of person who would not have let her suffer all day if he had been alive. As Jeannie says, "He *would* have found a way to call me!"

We have at least a few details of Al's last moments.

Cantor Fitzgerald is a high-powered brokerage firm where power and money are very important. Things like marriage, kids, and God can easily become a low priority. Many of Al's coworkers called him "the Rev," half out of affection, half making fun of him. They noticed, though, that he lived a different life. Al was very open with his colleagues about his faith and what God had done in his life. Some coworkers harassed him about his "morality," but they were usually the ones who also went to him privately to talk about marriage, work, or some other personal problem. They often asked him to pray for them, and he challenged them to also spend time in prayer themselves.

When the World Trade Center was bombed in 1993, Al was there helping his coworkers get down. It took three hours to get all the way down, and as people passed him in the halls they'd yell, "Hey, pray for us, Rev!" He'd respond by telling them that he had them covered! He stopped along the way and prayed with people who were upset or nervous. Even though some of his coworkers taunted him, they came to respect him and admired what he had.

In his last moments on September 11, 2001, Al continued his obedient journey to Christ. After the plane hit his tower that morning (according to spouses of some of Al's coworkers who died with him), "the Rev" got everyone in a circle, holding hands and praying. Some received the Lord for the first time. As usual, he thought of others more than he did of himself. He stepped into eternity, ready to meet his Lord face to face, bringing with him some of those he had prayed about for so long.

What a way to go. According to his family, he was not afraid to die, and this was a great way to go—serving the Lord in the middle of such a terrible time. He was able to help those who were with him to know a peace that goes beyond fear and pain.

His Christian Life

According to friends and family, Al Braca was a man who never wavered in his faith. He loved God with all his heart for 23 years—the length of his life as a Christian. He and his wife Jeannie both became Christians after they saw God heal their then 4-year-old daughter Christina of a rare blood disease. Although they had grown up going to church, neither Al nor Jeannie had made a personal commitment to Christ. Once they did, it was real and lifelong. Al was the kind of person who was very real about his faith, never falsifying the gospel by pretending that everything was okay when it wasn't! He knew that being a Christian didn't protect you from hard times. It meant that Christ gave you the faith and strength to get through those hard times.

Al's family was very important to him. He was proud of his children—older son David, twins Christina and Deanna, and younger son Christopher. By September 2001, David, Christina, and Deanna had married and had kids (Al had 3 grandkids and one on the way). Al's youngest child, Christopher, was in his junior year of high school. All of his children said about their father: "Our dad didn't yell at us a lot. He taught us right from wrong. He trusted us, and that made us not want to do the bad things that other kids seemed to be doing. He respected us and encouraged us all to have our own personal relationship with Christ and find our own calling in life."

They were taught that they couldn't be saved through their parents but had to make that decision on their own. Eventually, all of Al's children became Christians.

Deanna, one of the twins, admired her dad because he seemed to never waver in his faith and taught them that the most important things in life were a relationship with Christ and following His plan. She feels that her dad taught them to be faithful to God even when everyone around them is faithless. To follow God is the highest calling that anyone could have. Al and Jeannie also modeled a good marriage for the children.

Al was adventurous and included his family in that adventurous spirit. The kids were always exposed to things that would broaden their worlds. From traveling to seeing Broadway shows in the city, they did a lot together and saw the rest of the world!

He and Jeannie were proud of the way God had helped them raise their kids. They all have personal relationships with Christ and they had grown into good people! Al would be proud of them now.

Deanna said that although it has been very hard to not have their dad around, they have the promise of seeing him again in eternity because of their faith in Christ. Holidays and special days have been sad at times, but there is an inner peace that surpasses all understanding in their hearts and minds. God has been the Great Comforter for this whole family.

Al was a supportive and caring husband as well. He and Jeannie met as young people and had a friendship that took its time. When they got engaged, they stayed pure until marriage. They knew how important the marriage commitment was even at that young age. Al and Jeannie grew to know that in order to have a successful marriage, you must die to self. Jeannie remembers how much Al respected and loved her. She felt important to him—he seemed to make it his goal to show her that, often. According to Al and Jeannie's relationship, marriage is not a 50/50 compromise but a 100 percent giving of self and serving each other.

Al knew how to serve in his marriage. One way that Al served his wife was to care for her after she had a massive heart attack in the late 1990s. He came home from work each day and cooked, cleaned, and made sure the kids were ready for school the next day. Jeannie got better—a miracle herself, since she had only 16% of her heart's function left after the heart attack. She has been well since. She attributes it to Christ's healing in her life and her husband's sweet care.

A Churchman

At church, Al Braca was very active. An elder at his church, Calvary Chapel in Four Winds, New Jersey, Al was very involved in living out his faith. He took the role of elder very seriously. He prayed for the church and what they could do for Christ. He and Jeannie were the head of the Couples Fellowship. They loved these couples and prayed for them often. In the last seven months before he died, Al had begun ministering to a small group of men. There were some challenges going on in his church. He was called on to help and he stepped up to the plate. He had also just been chosen as a deacon, to serve others, a job he took very seriously.

Jeannie explains that Al believed their home should be a place where people could come and know Christ, whether that meant meeting Him for the first time or meeting Him as healer, comforter, counselor. Al tried to be the best friend and "brother" he could be to the men of the church. It was not unusual for them to have a breakfast Bible study or a baptism at the house. It was built for God, used by God, belonged to God. Early on, they had dedicated the house to God to be used for ministry; Jeannie continues with that commitment.

When Al ministered to others, they would often ask him to pray. When they did, he would ask them, "Did *you* pray about it, too?" If not, he'd tell them to go to the Lord first, pray, and them come back. He continued to direct others to God and not himself. He said that to everyone, including his family. Al was very concerned that people knew that their personal relationship with Christ was first and foremost!

A Christian at Work

Many people turned to Al for help at his job as well. There were times when Al wasn't sure about staying at his job, but he continued to feel called to stay and be an example to those he worked with. He respected the business but saw the hardships that came with being in a very power-driven, money-hungry business world. Al felt strongly that everyone should have the chance to have the gospel shared with them both in word and deed. He knew that he had a purpose, and even though there were times when he wanted to quit, he felt the Lord telling him to stay, so he did. He often called his wife and asked her to pray for him to get through a certain situation. Al wanted to be a light in the darkness, and he was glad that he could count on his family and church to encourage him in his calling, his job.

It is said that the way we conduct ourselves in a challenging time shows our true character. The character of

Christ certainly shone through many times in Al's life. He followed Christ with an obedient heart, and at the end of his life he stayed true to Christ.

Early in the morning of September 11, as Jeannie was having her quiet time, she asked the Lord to tell her what she should pray for. Her family came to mind. She prayed especially for her husband's protection that day, although that was her prayer every day. An impression that morning told Jeannie that God was going to "take Al home" that day. She dismissed it. As the morning went on, she learned of the planes hitting the trade center towers and heard that Al's building had been hit just below his office. She still thought he was safe but would be the last down because he was probably helping others. The kids were called together and they waited. Hope diminished for them as the second plane hit. When the towers fell, there was even more fear that he may have died.

Church friends gathered around the Braca family and brought comfort and strength that only those close to you can bring. According to friends, a pastor's wife who knew the Braca family had a dream the night of September 11. She dreamed that Al had been God's witness on the 104th floor, and that like Shadrach, Meshach, and Abednego, Jesus had been with Al through the fiery furnace he faced that day, and that he was not burned.

About a week later, Al's son went to the city to see if there was any chance of identifying his father. As the workers heard his description, they asked if he had certain characteristics and certain clothes, including a particular ring—and sure enough, Al's body had been preserved. According to reports, he was one of only 100 complete bodies found unharmed from the devastation of that day.

What can we learn from Al's life? A Scripture that was a favorite of Al's certainly speaks to his life. Proverbs 3:5–6 says this: "Trust in the LORD with all your heart and lean not on your own understanding; in all your ways acknowledge him, and he will make your paths straight." This is what Al lived. He trusted, acknowledged, and didn't lean on his own understanding. God walked with him all along his path and right into eternity, bringing with him some who learned in their last moments the truth that Al lived out in his life.

In Memoriam

LILLIAN CACERES

January 14, 1953 – September 11, 2001

2

LILLIAN CACERES

Devoted Angel of the Lord

The morning of September 11, 2001, when a plane hit Tower One of the World Trade Center, Lillian de la Cruz Caceres was in her office at Marsh & McLennan. She worked there as a technical analyst. She had gone to work early that day so she could be home when her daughter, Joanna, returned from her first day of school. The plane hit a floor near Lillian's office. She most likely died quickly.

On the evenings of September 9 and 10, 2001, Lillian was a part of a drama production at her church, Gateway Cathedral in Staten Island. It was an evangelistic drama about the frailty of life and how we can't know what the next day will hold. The scenes of the drama included a building collapse and a plane crash. Lillian portrayed an angel welcoming those whose names had been written in the Book of Life. Lillian left this world doing what she loved most, telling the good news of Christ.

Before each performance, Lillian prayed with the whole cast that the audiences would contemplate their own destinies and receive the message of Christ. After the play, according to Tim Mercaldo, one of the pastors at her church, Lillian spoke with someone who was thinking about making the decision to follow Christ. She told him that we don't know what tomorrow holds. Lillian left that night without knowing what an impact she had on him. Less than twelve hours later, she would be meeting her own destiny.

—·—

Lillian Caceres was a spunky, happy person who loved life and lived every day as if it were her last. If you had asked her why she was so joyful, she would have given direct credit to her relationship with Jesus Christ. Lillian did not have an easy life, so her testimony to God's strength, comfort, and power rang true. Her coworkers, family, and church friends say that she put others' needs above her own. Lillian truly cared about the people in her life and let them know it all the time through her actions and her words. Her death left a hole in many people's lives.

According to friends and family, Lillian was a bold witness who wasn't ashamed of her faith. She very lovingly shared who Christ was with others in many ways. She took seriously the call to tell the good news through song. Pastor Tim called her a "true minister of music" in that she was able to bring the love of God to others through her singing. On many occasions, Lillian received comments about how her singing ministered to a particular person.

Lillian was from a large family, which included her parents, four sisters, and five brothers. Her daughter, Joanna, brought the total to twelve. They were a close family, and Lillian was the fiber that held them together.

They miss her deeply and remember her acts of kindness toward them. Her brother Ruben says: "This past spring, my sister came and helped me after I contracted a paralyzing virus. She came every day and washed and fed me. She kept me company and even had time to meet some other patients and get to know them. . . . I don't know how she managed to do it all! She was a very good-hearted person. We lost an angel."

Lillian's parents remember their daughter as a tenderhearted person and a strong Christian. Other family members remembered that Lillian was always there for them, especially for special events. Her sister Hilda remembers when Lillian helped get her first job in Manhattan and gave her advice on getting around the city. The most important thing about Lillian, she says, was that she made her feel special—something she will carry with her for the rest of her life. Aurea, another sister, remembers how Lillian would make sure that she always had a great birthday, which was on Valentine's Day. Lillian would get her a big heart-shaped, rose-covered cake and invite Aurea's friends to celebrate. Family was very important to Lillian, and Lillian's family hopes that Joanna will remember that about her mom.

Many people remember Lillian as a woman of faith. She really lived out what she read in the Bible and took it not as a "suggestion" but as the truth. She saw her Lord as her friend and brother and lived to honor Him.

Four Things Lillian Would Say

As friends and family were interviewed, four things emerged that they feel Lillian would have wanted readers of her story to know.

You can never be too ready for what tomorrow will bring. In the Bible, James 4:14 says, "Why, you do not even know what will happen tomorrow. What is your life? You are a mist that appears for a little while and then vanishes." We don't know how much that "little while" includes for us. For Lillian it was 48 years. Make yourself ready by believing and living in the truth of Christ. He loves you. He accepts you as you are. He longs for you to know Him in a personal way. Not only does God want you to know Him personally, He wants to be with you for eternity.

Whatever pain you experience on this earth, it will all fade when you meet the Lord face to face. The pain we feel does come to an end one day. Lillian had experienced a lot of pain in her life. Some pain came from her own choices, some was inflicted by others, and some pain was just part of life. But in all of it, she had the hope that it would end one day and she would feel pain no more. In fact, the Bible says in Revelation 21:4, "He [the Lord God] will wipe every tear from their eyes. There will be no more death or mourning or crying or pain, for the old order of things has passed away." Lillian grew to know Christ in a more intimate way as she clung to Him during hard times. She found great peace and comfort from having a personal relationship with Him and knowing the "end of the story."

A church community is a vital part of a Christian's life. God never called His children to be Lone Rangers. Being a part of a church community helped Lillian get through some of the hardest times in her life. A church community can do far more together than one person can do on her own.

Live as a person who thinks of others' needs to be as important as your own. Lillian took care of others and put her own needs aside many times. Many people attest to her kindness and love toward others. Lillian apparently took heed of the words of Philippians 2:3–4 in the Bible, which says, "Do nothing out of selfish ambition or vain conceit, but in humility consider others better than yourselves. Each of you should look not only to your own interests, but also to the interests of others."

———

Lillian is in the presence of God now. Her tears are wiped away, and she sees God face to face. She is right where she would like to be. It was her goal in life to be able to honor God, and He must be saying to her: "Well done, My good and faithful servant." There is a void in the church choir and in her family's gatherings, but Lillian de la Cruz Caceres will live on in the hearts of those she touched.

In Memoriam

SUSAN HUIE

April 24, 1958 – September 11, 2001

3

SUSAN HUIE

"She Stood Out Like a Beacon"

No one would call Susan Huie ordinary. One
friend called her "a combination of Mother
Teresa and Jackie Kennedy." Along with being a
selfless, unusually giving person, this American-born Chinese forty-something single Christian woman had a keen
sense of grace and fashion—she always looked stylish
and dressed well.

Susan worked in marketing for Compaq Computers
in Manhattan. She didn't work at the trade center and
rarely went there. Her friends and family didn't know
that on September 11, 2001, she was preparing for a business meeting at the Windows on the World restaurant on
the top floor of Tower One of the World Trade Center.
Her voice mail simply said she would be out of the office
for a conference.

After the planes crashed into the towers, Susan's family had initially been more concerned about a church
member who worked at the WTC. They kept trying to
reach Susan and eventually were told that she had been
at the Windows on the World restaurant, right above

where the plane hit that ill-fated morning. Susan Huie, along with more than 3,000 other people, was presumed dead.

Her family and friends feel a great loss in their life. They also know that Susan made a great impression on everyone she knew, and that is to be celebrated. Susan's friends sent many notes of encouragement to her family. One thread running through all of them was Susan's big-heartedness. She poured her energy into living out what Christ taught in the Bible about letting your love be not just words, but actions as well (1 John 3:18).

Susan's coworkers at Compaq Computers, whether Christian or not, loved and admired her. They described her as caring and generous, and not your typical corporate person. She treated everyone at work with respect and dignity. She loved treating her coworkers with goodies and surprising them with things they liked. Not only did she shower them with treats so they would know someone cared, she listened and walked beside many who were facing personal crises. She was there for them, and although her responsibilities were important to her, people always came first. Friend and colleague Melissa Gordon said about Susan, "She was a person who worked with the best and brightest in the halls of world technology and finance, but she knew that the key to life's true essence was in personal relationships." Susan took seriously the talents and vocation that God had given her. Her goal was to one day be an executive. She always tried to do her best and worried that at times she hadn't done her utmost. She felt that quality work was a witness of her faith.

Some of her coworkers were influenced by her love for God. One in particular, Mark Bubar, said that Susan had influenced him in a quiet and natural way to attend church again after being away from it for a while. He never got to tell her that she had that influence on him. Another coworker said that Susan would stop by her desk frequently and remind her to take her children to church. Her influence will live on in them and others she knew at her job, at church, and everywhere she went.

———

Susan, who made a commitment to Christ at an early age, attended Chinese Evangel Mission in Manhattan's Chinatown. She was well loved and respected there. She taught Sunday school to young children and took it as a serious calling to lead them toward God. She had great influence on the children because she taught God's love not just by telling the Bible stories but by living out the meaning of those stories. She was consistent in telling them and showing them that she and God loved them, so that they would never forget.

The adults loved her just as much as the small ones did. She generated laughter, good hearty laughter, that brightened people's days. Susan would often go out after church to get food for the fellowship time. Several friends remember her bringing vegetables for the college students so that they could make fresh Chinese food during the week. She was called the "queen of care packages" because of her gifts to members of the church family who were away at school or in the military.

Susan's death has been very difficult for her family. It has been a painful time, and the gap in their family has been great. They will continue to miss her, grieve, and notice the hole at holidays and family gatherings, but they do have the same hope that Susan had, that as

Christ returns one day, they will be reunited with her in a glorious place.

Susan's family was very important to her. She and her dad, brother, and sister were close and shared many interests. She loved her nieces and nephews and took her role as "aunt" or "goo goo" (Chinese pet name for aunt) very seriously. She tried all she could to build them up and let them know how special they were as a creation of God.

Susan lived with her father and had cared for him for quite a while. They had a very special relationship. He adored his daughter and admired her for all she had done in her life, and he was proud of her and her faith in Christ. He spoke these words in her memorial book: "Not only did she contribute to large charities, but she gave so much to individuals. She was always thinking of other people."

Her brother Gordon remembers that Susan always reminded him to "pray for your marriage and for the Christian upbringing of your children." Gordon is thankful to Susan for reminding him of the priorities in life.

Pat, Susan's sister, said this to others in remembering Susan: "If there is anything you can do [in remembrance of Susan], be the friend to others that Susan was to you. Give of yourself unconditionally; look for opportunities to help others without expecting anything in return. Lend a hand or speak a kind word to someone in need. Susan would have wanted this."

Susan valued friendships as much as family. People were drawn to her because she reached out to others where they were. She didn't judge people for who they were or what they believed, but simply accepted and met them there. Her friend Judith Goodwin says, "Although I am not a Christian, she had the deepest respect for my religion and always expressed a sincere interest in my beliefs and life cycle events. Her attendance at my Bat Mitzvah was just one indication of how she respected me and others for who they were whether or not they believed in God."

———

Susan Huie was by no means perfect, but she was authentic. She had a special relationship with her Savior, Jesus Christ. She studied Scripture so that she would know how to please God. She loved as Christ loved, with acceptance of every person as a creation of God. She had integrity and dignity and knew her Source of hope and strength.

We don't know what Susan was doing in her last moments, but based on how she lived, we can suppose that she was helping someone or trying to make the best out of her situation. A coworker said about Susan, "When events turned uncertain or confusing, she stood out like a beacon of sanity, reasonableness, and positive thinking." We can hope that Susan had the opportunity to be that beacon on September 11, calming others and being a peaceful influence as they went to meet the Lord.

In Memoriam

JEFFREY LATOUCHE

November 22, 1951 – September 11, 2001

4

JEFFREY LATOUCHE

Prepared in His Spirit

Jeffrey LaTouche said goodbye to his wife and daughter at 5:00 A.M. and left his home in Brooklyn to go to work on September 11, 2001. He was a banquet manager for Windows on the World, a restaurant on the 106th floor of the World Trade Center Tower One, the North Tower. They were expecting about 300 guests for breakfast that morning. At 8:46 A.M., the first plane hit his building. Eventually, Jeffrey's body was recovered.

Jeffrey seems to have been given a discerning gift about his own destiny. Jeffrey's wife Virginia remembers that he was pensive and restless the week before the tragedy. At 49 years of age, he was usually full of energy and life. During that week, he wrote out instructions for his wife and family if anything were to happen to him. He cleaned his office and put everything in order. He told Virginia to get the brakes fixed on the car and register the car in her name only. It seemed that an inner spirit was telling Jeffrey to get life in order for his family, to make sure that they were okay. When Virginia went to his desk at home after he had died, she found his Bible open to

Isaiah 25. He had left it there the morning of September 11. Part of that chapter seemed to cry out about New York City on that day: "The city [is] a heap of rubble, the fortified town a ruin . . . . Surely this is our God; we trusted in him, and he saved us" (Isaiah 25:2, 9).

Jeffrey was born in Grenada but eventually moved to the United States and became a citizen. He married his wife Virginia in 1985. They have two daughters, Donna and Alina. Family was very important to Jeffrey, and he did his best to provide for them. Virginia will always be grateful for the time they had together. Their daughters will miss him greatly. They depended on their father not only for provision but for emotional support and advice as well. His daughters remember that he made birthdays and all special occasions very important. Virginia found a Mother's Day card that he had already bought for her . . . 9 months early. She and their daughters will always remember that about Jeffrey, and holidays will have something missing from here on out.

Church was one of Jeffrey's favorite places to be. He found the Lord and dedicated his life to Him in 1996. According to his wife and friends, Jeffrey made a drastic turnaround. He studied and sought the Lord and began to serve the Lord in many ways. Jeffrey and his family attended the Winners Chapel Church in Queens. He served as president of the men's fellowship, was on the church's building committee, and worked in the children's ministry. His pastor, Peter Kpapharo, says that Jeffrey was a fine and willing brother in Christ to many people.

In 2000, Jeffrey attended a men's conference and heard the evangelist T.D. Jakes. That conference seemed to change Jeffrey's heart. Virginia saw his spiritual eyes open up, and many things began to change even more. He had been active before, but he really got serious after that conference. His zeal and enthusiasm was so contagious that many noticed the change, especially his pastor. Jeffrey started his church on the process of acquiring a building with more space. The church continues to work toward the goal of $1 million for that building so they will have space to reach out even more than before.

As you read in Isaiah 25, it says, "O LORD, you are my God; I will exalt you and praise your name, for in perfect faithfulness you have done marvelous things . . . . You have been a refuge." Jeffrey LaTouche praised the Lord with his life. He is with the Lord now and is serving Him in love in heaven as he did on earth.

"He will swallow up death forever. The Sovereign LORD will wipe away the tears from all faces" (Isaiah 25:8). Virginia and her family and all of those who knew Jeffrey can rest on that promise. God will swallow up death and pain in the end, and they will see this special one who was loved by so many again one day.

In Memoriam

JENNIFER WONG

May 16, 1975 – September 11, 2001

5

JENNIFER WONG

Faithful Flower

Jennifer Wong was a beautiful young woman of 26 who loved to travel. Her nickname was "Fa Fa," the Chinese word for flower—an apt name for Jennifer, because she exuded the "aroma of Christ" as a young flower would on a sweet spring morning.

One of Jennifer's enjoyments was traveling. She went on short-term mission trips and fun trips as well. She had just returned from a trip to Italy on September 10, 2001. She and five other friends had enjoyed the history, the shopping, and the food of Italy, as well as just being together having a good time! Her friend Sandra noticed that during their trip, Jennifer got up every morning to have time alone with God. When they returned late on September 10, Sandra suggested they should all take off September 11 to catch up on sleep before heading back to work. But Jennifer decided to go to work that fateful morning.

On the crisp, sunny morning of September 11, Jennifer was at her desk at Marsh & McLennan in the North Tower of the trade center when the first of the two planes hit. According to reports and speculations, Jennifer probably died instantly, since the first plane hit near her office. Friends and family spent days looking for her, hoping that maybe she had not been in her office or had only been injured instead of killed.

After a week of checking hospitals and other places where she could be, her family and friends realized and accepted that Jennifer had died. Her memorial service a month later brought together more than a thousand people to remember Jennifer. Songs were sung and letters of love were read about her life. Even though it was a sad time, there was an air of hope that one doesn't always see at a funeral or memorial service. At the service were children in her Sunday school class at Chinese Evangel Mission in Manhattan's Chinatown, college friends, coworkers, and family. Many people told how Jennifer had shown them the kindness of Christ. Her brother Michael read a very tender letter he had written to Jennifer. Her life was a testament to what God could do when a person lets Him work through her.

One friend who knew Jennifer most of her life was Kenny Woo. He wrote this about Jennifer: "I give Jennifer credit for getting me to come to church regularly. When we were in high school, she and I were teaching Vacation Bible School together. One boy was not getting along with others. I was given the daunting task of setting him straight, but ended up making him cry instead. Jennifer redeemed the situation by talking to the boy and gently leading him to cooperate. Turns out this boy had a bad home life. Jennifer had the gift of patience to nurture him, and she helped him know God's love."

One college friend, Jason, wrote this about Jennifer: "The most important thing Jenn did for me was praying for my high school friends. I was very close to them, and

Jenn and I would pray for them by name. I recall that immediately after we started praying for them, we saw God working. Two of my friends were asking about God and really seeking. I had never really understood prayer, and she was showing me the power of prayer. A few years later, one of my friends came to know the Lord. The first thing I did was email Jenn. Another friend, Greg, told me on September 11, 2001, that he had become a Christian. I immediately thought of Jenn. When I found out that Jenn was missing, I emailed Greg and told him how Jenn had prayed for him." Many people said similar things about Jennifer. She cared about their concerns and truly believed that God would answer their petitions to Him.

Jennifer Wong was born into a Christian family but was taught that it was important to find her faith in her own way and her own time. Her parents, Ben and Joyce Wong, never forced their faith on their children; they just lived out what Christ taught. Jennifer saw that, and at age 11 she found her way into the Father's lap herself. Jennifer seemed to have a gift for demonstrating God's love to others in very tangible ways.

A business major, Jennifer planned to use her gifts to help people. She especially loved kids. When she graduated in May 1997, she delayed a job opportunity at a big New York bank to teach in Vacation Bible School again that summer, thinking it might be her last opportunity before she embarked in the working world. Thinking about her future and what it would hold, she wrote a poignant letter to God in her journal right after graduation.

Dear Lord,

As I begin to enter the workforce, I pray that I may not view the sacred and the secular with two different eyeglasses. I pray that I might view life through Your eyes. I am still unsure of the future, but with You I can do all things, Lord. Give me strong passions, Lord, so that I can be a full person, living for You and using the gifts that You have given me. Allow me to integrate my faith and work on all levels and remove the fears in my heart. Allow me not to be consumed by the idols I sometimes set up around me—wealth, greed, materialism, status. They really have no heavenly value. I offer all that I have to You. I pray that my life would not be free from trials and suffering but be full of Your teaching and grace and mercy. Let me live by Your Word as a living witness in all that I do. It gives me great comfort to know that You are in control of all things in my life.

Jennifer did become the person she had prayed to be. People wanted to be around her. Her best friend, Sandra Mark, commented that Jennifer intentionally spent time with her coworkers who were not Christians. She was just their friend and let God do the rest! Sadly, most of Jennifer's colleagues were killed along with her, so we are not sure if any became Christians. But we do know that God is faithful and that He used Jennifer in many ways to show His love to them.

When loved ones die, we sometimes think their influence stops. Not so with Jennifer. Many people have noted that Jennifer had some major effect on their lives even after her death. Sandra Mark notes that her friendship with Jennifer made her a better person. Jennifer's brother Michael cherishes the wisdom that she imparted to him in many areas of life. Several scholarships were started in her name to help others go to school.

One very important influence Jennifer had was on her friend, Cathy Lee. She and Cathy had been friends for about six years. Although Cathy had been to church events with Jennifer, she never accepted Christ as her Savior. After Jennifer's death, Cathy was in great pain, beside herself with grief. She saw that Jennifer's family all seemed to have peace, even in such terrible pain. During worship time at a winter church retreat, it all came together. Cathy felt an overwhelming sense that she needed to ask Christ to live in her. She wanted what Jennifer had. She asked Christ into her heart that night. She has been growing in the Lord, finding fellowship at church, and mentoring young people. She knows Jennifer was placed in her life to direct her to Jesus Christ. Even in her death, Jennifer influenced Cathy to know God.

The last week of Jennifer's life was spent enjoying Italy, being with good friends, and buying thoughtful gifts for her family back home. The night before her death, Jennifer spent time with her mom watching a favorite TV show that Joyce had taped for her, and they talked all about the trip. Joyce will always cherish that time. The last contact Jennifer's family had with her was the morning of September 11, when she and her sister Stephanie went in to work that day. As they parted ways to go to their office buildings, Jennifer said to Stephanie, "Where are you going?" Stephanie couldn't know that Jennifer was going to meet the One who loved her more than she could imagine, and would welcome her with open arms saying, "Well done, My good and faithful servant."

Read the story of Jennifer's sister, Stephanie Wong, also included in this book.

SECTION 2

FAITHFUL IN SERVICE

6

POLICE OFFICER BOBBY BAYER

Rushing to Ground Zero

New York City Police Officer Bobby Bayer is quiet and unassuming, a soft-spoken gentleman whose face conveys a sense of compassion and care. His love for his job outweighs the difficulties that come with being a police officer. He loves people and loves to help in times of need.

Before September 11, 2001, Bobby believed in God and called on Him through prayer, but going to church wasn't a priority for him. He did well at work, got to know the neighborhood pretty well, and people admired him. He, his wife Joyce, and son Bobby had a good life.

The morning of September 11, Bobby got to work early to catch up on paperwork. A group began gathering around the TV, so Bobby went to look. A plane (he thought it was a small aircraft, as most of the country did) had hit Tower One of the World Trade Center, about 4 miles from Bobby's precinct. The officers realized this wasn't an accident after a second plane hit Tower Two, and two more planes crashed into the Pentagon and a field in Pennsylvania. At the precinct, officers gathered and mobilized quickly. Bobby was in one of the first groups to be sent to Ground Zero, as it was now being called.

Bobby believes that as soon as they reached the precinct, God began working to keep him and his squad safe. As he looks back, he believes this day changed his relationship with God. He saw God become very real to him as a protector and as someone who cared about him in the scary moments.

The squad began their trek downtown. The first of many "miracles" was the delay that occurred as they stopped to pick up another officer—they had to wait because this person was late to the pickup point. As they drove on and got nearer the site, they were stuck in the horrendous traffic as people tried to leave the area—delay number two! After they parked their van a block away from the South Tower, they began walking toward the towers. As they got closer they saw debris falling and realized that it was human bodies—people were jumping from the towers. Bobby remembers thinking how these people must have been so frightened to choose to end their life instead of letting the fire end it for them. He became incredibly sad.

Bobby's commander realized that not everyone had their protective gear, so they all headed back to the van to get it. As they were getting their gear, Bobby heard a low rumbling sound. He looked up and saw the south tower shift. He said out loud, "This thing is going to fall! We have to get out of here!" As they all ran, it seemed like minutes passed, but it was just seconds later that the tower fell. A huge cloud of dust came after them.

Bobby stayed just ahead of the cloud until he saw a lady who had fallen down. He stopped to help her up and the cloud of debris caught up with him. He felt as if someone had turned the lights off of a bright, sunny day. He got the lady to safety and continued running toward where he thought his buddies were. He caught up with some of them and they began to try to regroup a few blocks away. Then the second tower fell, and there was more dust and debris. This cloud was going the opposite direction from them, so the second cloud that hit Bobby wasn't as intense as the first.

There was so much chatter on the radios that they couldn't call three of their group who had been sidetracked. Bobby remembers a lot of chaos around them. People seemed mesmerized and either couldn't move or were running away. The guys went into a drugstore across the street. They found the only phone in the area that was actually working. He got the associate there to keep calling his wife to get the message to her that he was okay. He was very grateful to have found a phone and that the kind lady helped him get a message to his wife. He thanked God for her later! The rest of the group got on the phone and tried to find the others who had strayed away. Not really knowing what to do next, they began to direct pedestrian traffic. Bobby describes the whole day as like a cartoon, with everyone scrambling around yet seeming to be in slow motion.

Along with others, Bobby worked about 15 hours that day. Later that night, in the darkness around Ground Zero (all electricity was out except for floodlights at the site) they went to find out what had happened to the van. They found it virtually untouched, the doors open as they had left them, no glass broken, no tires blown out. All around them cars were scorched and crushed; the police van was full of ash but intact. As they drove out of the area, they saw desks and filing cabinets and computers all around them, lots of debris and very few human beings. Bobby describes it as ghostlike.

Most of the officers, including Bobby, spent the night at the precinct. Bobby woke up with breathing trouble and had to go to the hospital. He was diagnosed with severe asthmatic symptoms, given medication, and sent to his regular doctor. More than a year later, he still suffered with breathing problems.

Because of his breathing problems, he was given desk duty and not allowed to go back down to Ground Zero. Watching fellow officers go there, he got depressed and felt as if he wasn't doing anything worthwhile. For a long time it was very hard. He also suffered from some post-trauma through nightmares, depression, and ongoing health problems. When he got to go to the site months later, that was difficult as well. All the memories came flooding back.

What did Bobby learn in all this? He saw God like never before. He knew about God all his life but had never really "experienced" God and His love. He believes God has sustained him through this hard couple of years. He saw God at work through the restaurant owners who brought food to the precinct every day for months, losing income in an already hurting economy. He saw God in the Christian chaplains who came from all over the country to listen to and serve all the officers, no matter what they believed. Bobby has seen God in the new relationships he has built in one of the Christian churches in the community, and he has seen God in his own life, keeping him safe from harm that day and every day.

Bobby doesn't know why God chose to spare his life, and he may never know until he sees Christ face to face.

But he does feel it is important to live with gratefulness every day for the future, whatever it may hold. Bobby is sure that God is there for Him, going ahead of him to guide him in life.

Bobby celebrated his 20th anniversary as a police officer in early 2003—he celebrated by retiring on the same day he started his job with the NYPD. He looks forward to spending more time with his family. He feels that his faith in God will help him to find what to do next in his life. This is a new chapter of life for Bobby Bayer, and he is excited at the possibilities, knowing he is not alone.

7

POLICE OFFICER LORY FINOCCHARIA

Empowered by God's Strength

L ory Finoccharia is a bundle of energy and has a thick, jovial New York accent. She loves her job— she has been a New York City police officer for 16 years and looks forward to coming to work each day. Lory sees every person she meets as an opportunity to show God's love. This is a calling for her, not just a job, and that sense of calling helps her to cope with the hard things she has experienced.

Lory became a Christian at age 19 and immediately saw God move in her life. She spent a year as a missionary for Youth With A Mission and worked in Washington state, Hawaii, and Japan. Lory uses her beautiful voice to praise the Lord and minister to others through song. After a couple of years, she came back to New York and soon was married. She and her husband, Mike, live in Orange County, NY, with their children Brian, Aja, and Dakota.

Before September 2001, Lory had a strong faith and knew God was in control of her life. She went to church regularly and often prayed with her partner at work. Yet she felt stagnant in her Christian growth and longed to know God in a deeper way. Little did she know that God would provide plenty of opportunity for growth over the next year and a half.

On the morning of September 11, Lory was visiting with her dad on his birthday, having a cup of tea. Her husband called to tell her that the twin towers had been hit. She turned the TV on and couldn't believe her eyes! Knowing she needed to get to work immediately, she arranged to drive in with some other female police officers who live near her, gathered a sleeping bag and a few other necessities, and left. She stopped at an aunt's house to pray before she got on the road. During the hour drive into the city, she and the other female officers pondered what must be playing out in the city. Lory remembers praying out loud and feeling an immediate peace in her heart. She knew then that she would be okay and that she could leave her family in God's hands.

Lory did security all that first day, guarding the precinct's block because no one knew what else might happen. She spent much of that day praying. Lory worked security at different places during the next weeks—the city was on high alert for quite a while. There were many intense hours, and she began to feel extremely fatigued. As the weeks went on, she spent time at Ground Zero, and she would never forget what she saw. She finds it hard to put into words the devastation that was around her. Each morning she would wake up exhausted and emotionally fatigued from the difficult work and the 12 to 15 hour shifts. She repeated this prayer through her fatigue: "Lord, I know You will give me strength to do this because I can't on my own. I will get through this because it won't go on forever." Lory found the strength she needed for each day, and as time went on, she began to experience God's love in new and fresh ways.

Lory experienced God's love through many people. The thousands of cards sent, the people cheering them on as they left the site each day, the food, the love, the chaplains who came to help, all these encouraged and lifted her up. Every time she thought she wouldn't make it, someone gave her a hug or thanked her, and she was revived. Tears often spilled out because she felt as if those touches and kind words were God in flesh. A new and fresh trust in the Lord came and surprised Lory. He helped her through days when she saw families hurting deeply. These were the days that knowing God really mattered.

Since September 2001, Lory has had ups and downs. She has dealt with anger, sadness, and the emotional toll of a terrorist attack. Her family was affected as well, but thanks to the many who prayed for them, they have grown closer.

One special person, Police Chaplain Dan Lovin, came from Illinois to New York to help. He reached out to Lory and her family and has kept in touch with them since the attacks. He always seemed to show up at the right time, whether through email, a surprise visit, or a phone call.

Lory and her husband have gone to Christian marriage retreats for 9-11 recovery workers and attended a crisis intervention debriefing, and each time that she talks it out, she feels a little closer to "normal." She knows that she will never be exactly the same again, but that is good in many ways. New career opportunities are opening, and her family is closer. Some churches near her work offered help, and now she has a place to find support on hard days.

Lory knows that without Jesus in her life she would not be where she is now. She has a stronger sense of calling, and so have some other Christian officers. Her faith is different now. For Lory, faith means "trusting in God with everything in your life. Then you don't have to know everything. Even when life is difficult like September 11, God will get you through it. You can trust Him and who He says He is in all the chaos of life."

When asked what she would say about God, September 11, and faith, she responded: "Times are coming when we all will need to decide which path in life we are going to follow—God's path to life or the one that leads to destruction and eternal separation from God. If you are a Christian believer, it's important to walk your faith, not just talk it. You never know whom you will influence. If you are not a believer, get to know who God is through the Bible. He will never let you down even when devastating things happen like September 11. I think God was able to use this opportunity to bring us back to Him. He didn't cause it but because of free will, He allowed it to happen. Many, many people ministered to me and reached out to me. I saw God in the arms that reached out and the food that was served. I saw God love me and be more personal to me because I let Him. Let God love you . . . ."

Lory really will never be the same. She is not at a standstill in her faith anymore. She loves God and will follow Him wherever He leads. Some Bible verses a friend shared mean a lot to her: "Although the Lord gives you the bread of adversity and the water of affliction, your teachers will be hidden no more; with your own eyes you will see them. Whether you turn to the right or to the left, your ears will hear a voice behind you, saying, 'This is the way; walk in it'" (Isaiah 30:20–21).

8

POLICE OFFICER BRIAN O'NEIL

"Jesus, Jesus, Jesus"

Brian O'Neil loves being a New York City police officer. Brian is a youth officer at a precinct in Manhattan and sees his job as a ministry to teenagers that church youth ministers may not be able to reach. He works in local high schools with youth who have difficulties, responds to gang-related incidents, and teaches youth crime prevention so that teens have a fighting chance to make better decisions. It would be easy to get cynical in his job; Brian fights that all the time. But because of the commitment he made a few years ago to a personal relationship with Jesus Christ, he is able not only to work with youth but to pray for them along the way.

Although Brian attended church and read the Bible, he had never read it closely until he began to read it with his partner on patrol. His partner, a Christian, often suggested Scriptures relating to issues Brian faced in his personal life and with teenagers he met. As he read, he began to see God in a new light, a more personal one. As

Brian talked to his partner and sought God, he came to a personal knowledge of Jesus as Lord and Savior. Thanks to the Holy Spirit and a patient partner, Brian came to that full knowledge in his heart.

Early in 2001, as Brian was taking the commuter rail line from Manhattan to his hometown in upstate New York, the train began to derail. The cars jerked back and forth; people and their belongings were flying to and fro. He realized that this was serious. He began to pray a prayer that would become his favorite, especially when he didn't know what else to say: *Jesus, Jesus, Jesus.* As he prayed, he felt a peace coming over him that he had never experienced. The train slowed down and Brian got out unharmed. He didn't know how to deal with that at first, but took it as a sign of God's love and protection for him. Brian has no doubt that there are "angels unseen" as he goes about his business of protecting the city and helping teenagers stay out of trouble. Little did he know he would experience God's protection again just months later, and those simple words would get him through a tragedy that he could never imagine.

September 11, 2001, began as one of the ten most perfect weather days of that year. There wasn't a cloud in the sky, and the temperature was topping 80 that day with low humidity. Brian came in to work early because he had duty with the mayoral primary elections being held that day. He heard on the news at the station that a plane had crashed into the World Trade Center. Like everyone else, he thought a small plane had accidentally crashed.

Because of his position as non-essential personnel, Brian is usually mobilized as one of the first on the scene, but this time he wasn't. He was on regular patrol duty with another colleague that day, assigned to the West Side Highway, a major thoroughfare to the World Trade Center. From his position about 4 miles away from the WTC, he could see the tragedy unfold before his eyes!

Brian was assigned to re-direct traffic off the highway. He would have preferred to be at the trade center, helping. From his post at the top of the highway, he saw the flames and then the towers collapsing. All he could do was pray the words that kept coming to his mind: *Jesus, Jesus, Jesus.* He felt very alone and afraid because he knew that when the towers came down he lost many friends and colleagues. He knew that some of his own precinct buddies might also have been killed in those moments. (Brian sees now that he could have been down there himself if he had not been reassigned).

Brian shifted his focus to the people arriving in his area, running from the trade center using the only means of transportation available, their feet. They were covered with dust from head to toe and had shocked looks on their faces. The only thing he could do to help was open the hydrants and give them water to drink and to wash off. He then took their names, more out of a comfort to them than any real assistance at that moment. Brian felt helpless, but at the same time these little acts of kindness seem to relieve their shock just a little bit. He promised himself that he would pray for them. That was all he could do in that moment, pray and give water.

That evening, about 11 P.M., Brian returned to the station. He found out that all his precinct coworkers had survived the collapse because they had forgotten their helmets and were ordered to go back to the van and get them. This is one of many miracles that Brian would see over the months ahead.

About 3 A.M. on September 12, Brian was assigned to the temporary morgue. The day passed quickly and grimly. It was an experience that he would never be able to talk about. Seeing his fellow New Yorkers either burned or torn apart to the point of being indistinguishable left him speechless. He was glad that some bodies had been found; he knew it was important for the families' closure. But the experience was one he would never wish on anyone.

During the next three days, Brian worked on the bucket brigade, pulling body parts and personal items out of the rubble. He continued to pray *Jesus, Jesus, Jesus* as he sifted through remains. There was some hope in the beginning for recovery of live persons, but hope quickly diminished as no one was being found alive. Those three days were very stressful. The stability of buildings surrounding the site had been compromised, and whistles were frequently blown, signaling workers to leave the site because of risk that a building might collapse. Workers would often get a possible human scent from the NYPD canines but then would have to leave because of a whistle. After the all-clear they might not be able to locate the scent again. That was extremely frustrating to all involved. Brian was overwhelmed at the loss of life and just continued to pray *Jesus, Jesus, Jesus*.

Over the next six months, Brian was at Ground Zero about once a week. He began to see acts of God, both in his personal life and his surroundings. The chaplains on-site who reached out to him and his colleagues were wonderful, and he saw colleagues come to know Christ. Workers began to receive kind notes and cards from people all over the world, and he began feeling something he had never felt before . . . the love of God through complete strangers. One morning as he was leaving the work site, a large Rastafarian gentleman came toward him with arms open wide. Brian was a bit taken aback, since the Rastafarian culture is so different to him. The guy came up and said, "I love ya, mon," and hugged him so tightly that Brian couldn't breathe. In those moments, he saw how God uses the oddest circumstances to give us His love. Brain felt as if God hugged him that day through the Rastafarian man. The generosity and kindness of strangers overwhelmed him, and Brian began to feel God, in his heart, telling him that He was loving him through others, even people he did not know.

Brian learned that Scripture can be a real comfort, especially when you can't find the words to speak. One such Scripture that became very special to him as he was working on "the pile" (this was the nickname for the debris at Ground Zero, which had become a pile of rubble) was Isaiah 43:1–2: "Do not fear . . . I have called you by name; you are Mine! . . . When you walk through the fire, you will not be scorched, nor will the flame burn you." Brian literally watched his shoes burn and melt from the hot debris he walked on at Ground Zero.

Every day as Brian went to Ground Zero, there was an outpouring of love on the highway going out of the site, and that was incredible to him. Brian had always thought that people saw police in New York City as zeroes, not heroes, but that had changed instantly. Brian has always tried to be the best police officer he can be. He is even more committed today, as he has seen God work in and through many police, firefighters, and civilians. So many people in the community have come together, and that is exciting to Brian.

It is sometimes more difficult to receive love than to give love, especially for one who prides himself in being strong. Brian is learning to receive love now, and that has made him a better police officer. He sees people in the community in a different light and tries hard each day to live a life that is pleasing to God. He wants to be a light in the midst of a city that is filled with darkness. He wants the kids he works with to know what he knows, that God loves them and is with them through good times and bad.

Brian has faith in God that he had not had before September 11, 2001. These days, Brian has a more intimate relationship with Jesus, relies more on Him, loves others more, and is more of an outspoken witness to his colleagues as well as teenagers he sees every day. Brian saw Christ stand strong for Him on days when he couldn't carry on. This tragedy, in Brian's words, "sealed the deal" for him concerning his own relationship with the Lord Jesus.

9

POLICE OFFICER HEIDI RIZZO

Finding Christ in the Love of Relief Workers

While driving home after taking her daughter to school, Heidi Rizzo heard on the radio that a plane had hit the World Trade Center. At first she thought the deejays were playing a bad joke, but other stations were reporting the story as well. Heidi knew immediately that she would be called in to work, but she didn't know that in the coming months her life would change drastically and she would meet God in an unusual place . . . an abandoned airfield parking lot used for food preparation for the recovery workers at Ground Zero.

Heidi is a police officer for the New York City Police Department, and she usually worked with juveniles. On September 11, she wanted to help with the recovery efforts and to be in the middle of the chaos, helping find people. She was assigned a position that was not exciting at all. She was assigned to security at an abandoned airfield east of Manhattan, almost out of the city, in southeastern Brooklyn. She and a few other officers provided security for volunteers cooking food for the recovery workers. No fast action! No bodies recovered! What were they thinking? Heidi was frustrated to be there, working 12-hour shifts at a place where the subway didn't go and not much traffic came their way.

However, Heidi shifted her attitude and found opportunities to support and care for those who came to the site, listening to them and being a caring presence for them. She and her fellow officers also started answering hundreds of cards sent to encourage them by children all over the world. That helped her to feel productive.

As time went on, Heidi began getting to know the volunteers who came through. She met many nice folks, and particularly got to know volunteers from Kentucky's Baptist Disaster Relief Team. She was amazed that these folks had given up their time and money to come and be there for New Yorkers. What was it that made them do this? She got curious and asked them what they believed. These volunteers shared with her about their personal relationships with Jesus Christ. Heidi felt her angry heart soften as they told her what God had done in their lives. That was why they were serving Him here. They were here to share God's love in a tangible way with those who were hurting. Heidi remembers them sharing it in such a simple way that she understood how much God loved her. They asked her if she wanted to be a Christian and share in that love, and she said yes! She prayed and dedicated her heart and life to Jesus that day.

Through the next year and a half, Heidi has seen God work in her and through her. She has been thrilled that her Kentucky friends have kept in touch. She is meeting other Christians and growing in the Lord. She knows that if she has a question, she can go to the Bible and seek the answer. She has struggled over why all of this happened in September 2001. She now sees that even when dark things happen in our lives, God can bring good out of it. The neat thing for Heidi has been that she can take her everyday problems to God and He will help her, not only when there is a massive terrorist attack but even when simple everyday problems occur.

Heidi's faith has helped her trust God even with the anger she felt because so many died on September 11. Faith has meant being able to get through memorial service after memorial service for her colleagues and seeing the deep grief felt by many. Faith means that life has meaning and purpose and that her job is not just a job, but also a way to show God's love in tangible ways. Faith means that God is there with you 24 hours a day and 7 days a week, whether times are good or bad.

10

POLICE OFFICER BOBBY RICE AND KIM RICE

A New Family in Christ

Bobby Rice: Kneeling at Ground Zero

Bobby Rice, a police officer with the Port Authority of New Jersey, had no idea that he would find Christ in the midst of the rubble at Ground Zero. Bobby lives in southern New Jersey and is trained in crisis counseling. When the attacks of September 11 occurred, Bobby offered to help. On September 11, Bobby went to the trade center to counsel the Port Authority officers. They ended up calling in volunteer chaplains from various places—to add manpower, and also because people were asking, "Do you have a chaplain, a priest, a rabbi up there?"

Bobby felt then that he had no need for religion. He remembers on the day of the attacks getting ready to go in a church and thinking, *I still have no need to walk into a church. I haven't needed a church for almost 40 years—what's it gonna do for me now?* He remembered movies where people who had never been religious would call out to God on their deathbeds. Bobby felt that was being a hypocrite—and he didn't want to be a hypocrite.

The Volunteer Chaplains

As work went on at Ground Zero, Bobby started getting to know the chaplains. The first chaplain he met was Ricky Hargrave, a Baptist pastor from McKinney, Texas. Then a group of chaplains from San Bernardino, California, came in. Bobby hit it off immediately with three chaplains named Greg, Ron, and Gary. He watched the chaplains work with police officers, construction workers, firemen, military, National Guard, and volunteers. He watched them talking to anyone who needed to talk.

The chaplains handed out American Bible Society pamphlets made especially for workers at Ground Zero, saying, "I'd like you to read this when you have time." As they talked to people, Bobby would often stand back and observe, seeing the chaplains put their arms around someone, bow their heads, and pray with them. He remembers chaplain Gary telling him, "It's incredible—a guy was just saved out in the middle of the pile there." That was the first time Bobby had ever heard the word *saved* used that way. He thought of "saved" in the sense of people's lives being saved, like from a terrorist attack. He had never known anything about souls being saved. That was when they started chipping away at the hard exterior Bobby didn't even know he had.

Bobby says Gary would correct him when he used bad language, giving him replacement words for the foul words. Bobby comments, "Sometimes my partner and I would forget they were around and we'd apologize for our language, but they took it in stride and didn't get upset." Bobby says that another thing God did through these guys was change their behavior concerning women! Gary saw Bobby grinning and making comments about some of the cute college-age girls handing out water and sandwiches at the site—noticing their midriff shirts and "accidentally" getting video of them. One day Gary noticed in Bobby's truck a picture of Bobby's wife, Kim. Gary said, "You know Bobby, I don't understand something. Let me ask a question: what kind of food don't you like?" Bobby answered, "That's easy— Chicken McNuggets. I can't even stand to smell them." Gary said, "When those girls walk by, I watch your head turn. Try thinking of them as Chicken McNuggets. I see this picture of your wife—you got prime rib." Bobby laughed it off. But then every time a girl would walk by, he'd turn his head and there would be Gary, saying, "Chick-en Mc-Nug-gets." Bobby explains, "Finally it started taking effect on me—I stopped looking as much. And eventually it stopped totally. That was just Gary and God working on me the whole time I was in there."

A Special Recovery

One particular recovery was a spiritual experience for Bobby. He helped recover Port Authority Officer Clinton Davis—they didn't know his name at the time—on September 23 at about 3:30 A.M. His body was found in the staircase of Tower Two, wedged between steel. The only way to get his entire body out was to cut it in half. The lieutenant asked Bobby which half he thought the family would prefer to have. Bobby says, "We all prayed together, and I said I think the family would be happy with whatever half they could bring out of their loved one." When they started cutting, a gas pocket in the body deflated and they were able to bring the whole body out.

They sent a basket by crane, put his body in the basket with a flag over it, and brought it out. Bobby says, "Two Port Authority officers were lowering his body into a box, and we started to move away. When we did, the PA officers put their arms around us and pulled us back in and motioned for us to stay there. They let us be part of this very intimate recovery of one of their officers." The recovery of Officer Davis was very emotional for Bobby's group—they wear his name on bracelets to this day.

Bobby says, "I see the signs, the miracles, the doors the Lord opens for me." He was surfing the Internet and found an article on Port Authority Officer Jarrett, who turned out to be Clinton Davis's best friend. He contacted Jarrett, feeling he had to know more about Clinton Davis, what kind of person he was, what he was all about.

Bobby was invited to the Christmas party for children of officers who had died. As he helped carry the presents to the party, he looked down at a gift in his hands, and the tag read, "Clinton Davis, Jr." The Davis family didn't show up that day, but Bobby was able to meet Mrs. Davis in the fall of the next year. He says, "It was an honor to share the story with her and tell her how important her husband was for us. God is good!"

In late November, Bobby brought his wife Kim to the trade center to meet his chaplain friends Gary, Ron, and Greg. Greg and Ron were leaving the next morning. So Gary said to Bobby, "Why don't you go to church with us? I'm going to go meet with an NYPD officer." Kim and Bobby went with them to Harvest Fellowship Church— by that point, Bobby says, he wanted to go to church. The church looked like a dance studio, with mirrors and a bar on the walls—but it had a worship team, and people were in jeans. Bobby and Kim felt really comfortable and liked the church.

As they were driving home, Kim said to Bobby, "I know why you come back now. I never understood why you would want to come back." They had taken her down into the pit at Ground Zero. She had seen how the officers, the chaplains, and everybody were like a big family after three months of spending almost 24 hours a day together. "It was really neat to hear her say that," Bobby says.

"Finish What I Started"

On Chaplain Gary's last night, December 8, he and Bobby made a lot of recoveries. It was a great ending for Gary before he went home. The next morning was an emotional goodbye. By that point Gary knew Kim, so Bobby put her on the phone and they were all crying. They had a bond, a friendship, that Bobby knew was for a lifetime. Bobby spoke to Gary a couple of times during layovers on his flight home. At one point, Bobby mentioned, "Gary, I saw Ricky Hargrave tonight." Ricky was the first chaplain Bobby had met at Ground Zero. They weren't particularly close because Ricky was working at the morgue. Gary said to Bobby, "Tell Ricky to finish what I started with you." Bobby didn't know what he meant.

Here's the rest of Bobby's story in his own words:

It was a rough night sleeping. I woke up the next morning, and it was like a light bulb had gone off in my head. I knew exactly what I wanted. I can't tell you what happened that night, but I knew right then and there. I went back and asked where Ricky was. My friend Roland told me that he was getting ready to go out on the pile. I told

Roland that I needed to talk with him; he says, "What's this all about?" I said, "It's personal." When Roland heard that, he says, "All right"—because at some point we all needed to talk about what we were doing up there. I guess he figured I needed to get something off my chest.

So I found Ricky. I told him that I needed to talk to him. He says okay, so we went to an old office. And Ricky's like, "What's going on?" And I said, "I talked to Gary last night and he said to tell you to finish what he started." Ricky said, "Are you ready?" I said, "I'm ready, just tell me what to do." So we knelt down right there at Ground Zero. He recited a prayer, and I repeated it after him. My whole life changed right then, like a 180-degree turn. After that, we finished praying and gave each other a hug. I had cried before about what I saw up there, but this was a different type of tears. Then I heard a voice coming out of my telephone—to my surprise, my phone had dialed Greg while we were praying! I said, "Greg, you're not going to believe what happened!" He said, "Yes, I do, I heard the whole thing! It's great!"

What is exciting is that since I have become a Christian, my wife and I started attending church, and our two boys have become Christians. We have all been baptized and joined a great church near our home. The pastor and members are so welcoming and wonderful and have helped us to grow in our faith. God loves us and we love Him more than ever! Who would have guessed?

Kimberly Rice: God, My Heavenly Father

God works in unusual ways. Through her husband Bob's experience at Ground Zero, Kim Rice of southern New Jersey came to a more personal relationship with Jesus Christ. That was a great event, and it certainly changed her life. September 11 was a horrible time, but for people like Kim, that day began a good work in her husband and her family. Her husband Bob is a Port Authority Police Officer in Southern New Jersey. She shares her faith walk here.

—·—

I was always very—I don't want to say religious—but I've always prayed. I was saved when I was a teenager. God has always been a part of my life, but never so much as now, since the September 11 attacks. That Tuesday night, the night of the attacks, I went to a memorial service. I wasn't a member of the church and I didn't know anyone there—I was just going because I felt I needed to.

I went in and there was an elderly lady who lived down the street from us. She had lost her husband a few months before. She was sitting there in the back, all by herself. I sat next to her and held her hand, and she said, "Kimmy, you are such an angel." She was sitting there praying that the Lord would show her what to do, where to go from here. She was really scared and was really glad that I walked in. I went home with such a peaceful spirit that night. It was just a great time of prayer—really neat. I feel that God had begun a work in me a long time ago, but this memorial service was a new beginning to a deeper relationship with Christ.

It's really different now. It's personal. It's not just that God is there—He is my God, my Savior, and my world.

That is what is so cool to me. Once I let go and turned over my heart fully to Him, I saw what it was all about. I'm full of peace, and my whole family is full of peace, and that is the best thing for us. We needed that so much. I can see how God has been there all my life. So much more comes to light once you really, truly open your eyes.

I see that September 11 really started God's work in my family and me once again. When Bob became a Christian, it was as if our whole world changed. Our boys have come to know the Lord, and it is even spreading out to some extended family as well.

One of the greatest things Jesus has done for our family is heal our son, Bobby. After September 11, he had been coming home late a lot—and just off the wall things told me something was not right. So I went through his bedroom and found five empty bottles of rum. That just blew me away. He's only 15, and I was at my wit's end. His dad was in New York working at the pile, and I was home by myself.

We took Bobby to a therapist, and he suggested we get him hooked up in an alcohol rehab near us. I picked him up every day after school and took him for his two-hour session. That was a really tough time. His brother Michael would come home by himself after school; he was 12 at the time. Michael was like, "Why is this happening to us? Daddy's in New York, you're taking Bobby to rehab, and he is drinking." Everything was just such a mess. And this went on for a while.

I kept thinking that I needed my husband here. He's their father, he's my husband, and we needed him here—why was he working down at the pile and not even getting paid for it? Well, once I got the opportunity to be there, it was overwhelming. They took me to the site, and I just sobbed and sobbed. I have never seen anything so void in all my life. And that was after a lot of cleanup was done. It was incredible.

Bob became a Christian on December 9. Everything began to change then. My husband used to speak like a truck driver—that even started to change. Our kids could see a change. Even the neighborhood kids could see a change—wow, what happened to Mr. Rice? Our chaplain friends who helped him find Christ took us to church in the city, and we loved it. We knew that soon we would need to find a church closer to home, so we got references and found a great fellowship soon after that. Bob had finished up a midnight shift shortly after Christmas, and he came home early that Sunday and said, "I found the one! Will you get up and go with me?" So we went and left the boys a note on the computer saying that we had gone to church!

We wanted the kids to be involved in church, but we knew Bobby might be resistant, so we decided to let God work in his life. At first it was just the two of us going to church, then Michael came, then Bobby. They had a youth group on Wednesday night, so we took the kids and they actually started going.

Even the teachers at school have seen a change in Bobby. His whole attitude, his whole disposition has changed. He finally got to the point. He started out saying, "I don't want to go to church." Well, there was a girl there, and she was really pretty, and she started talking to Bobby. And I said, well, you know, whatever it takes! At that point, everybody was going to church and things started to get more peaceful, easier at home.

I lost my dad to leukemia in 1999. It's kind of like God has taken the place of my earthly dad. I used to talk to my dad—oh, well, this is happening, that's happening. Now I have a personal relationship with Christ. It's like, well hey, this is going on, that's going on. What do You want me to do here? There?

I have always believed that everything happens for a reason. God has a master plan. There's no use crying over it—just pick up the pieces and go on. For instance, during the time Bob was working in New York—there is no way on my own I could have taken care of Bobby, gotten him through this treatment, and saw so many changes on my own power! That was God; that had nothing to do with me. That was God leading me—to the therapist, to the youth group, because they've been there and they know what he's going through.

Bobby was saved on his teen retreat and baptized on a mission trip to Mexico. Michael has come to a peace about things now. And now my sister has started coming to church with me because Calvary Chapel has a women's study. I invited her, and she came, and she's still there. She's a single parent, has two kids. This has transformed my entire life.

God brought much good out of this horrific situation. I'm learning to trust the Lord for my family's well being and for their safety. The verse that I memorized first was Ephesians 2:8— "For it is by grace you have been saved, through faith—and this not from yourselves, it is the gift of God." I started learning that one in September of 2001 after the attacks. This year, I'm learning and studying Romans 8:28— "And we know that in all things God works for the good of those who love him, who have been called according to his purpose." When September

11 happened, we did not realize that God was going to use this opportunity to share His love with us in such a tangible way! We are amazed at how He knew what we needed, when we needed Him. If anyone has any doubt that there is a God, let them come and be with our family and let us tell you where we have been and what life is like now. He has filled a void in our individual lives as well as our family life. We know our Source of help and strength to now face whatever comes our way!

11

FIREFIGHTER KEN HESSEL

Firefighting Pastor

Ken Hessel of Westbury, New York (a suburb on Long Island), is pastor of Redeemer Lutheran Church. He does the typical pastoral things: hospital visits, Sunday sermons, study, and repairs around the church building. Ken is unique, though, because he is not only a pastor, but a firefighter as well. He serves as a volunteer firefighter in the town of Westbury. It's not unusual to see him, day or night, hanging onto a fire truck, rushing on his way to help someone.

Pastor Ken sees firefighting as going hand-in-hand with his calling to pastor. Part of being a Christian is heeding Jesus' command to "love your neighbor as yourself," which means you help your neighbor when they are hurting, or when their house is burning. To save whatever they can, especially loved ones, means a great deal to Ken and his fellow firefighters. Ken says that he sees God working through firefighting in small but significant ways.

Ken, his wife Theresa, and their kids Kaalleen and Erik were shocked when the planes crashed into the

World Trade Center on September 11. Ken's fire department was immediately called out to serve at Ground Zero. He shared emails with people during the days that followed, keeping them updated and urging people to pray. Here are some selections from his emails.

Wednesday morning, September 12, 2001

It is now 3:30 A.M. and I have just returned from Ground Zero, what was once the World Trade Center. As many of you know, in addition to being a pastor I am a volunteer firefighter. Our department was called to stand by and assist FDNY (Fire Department of New York) as needed. At around 5 P.M. on 9-11-01 our unit was directed to go down there. Our first orders were to help stretch some hose lines to equipment that was already there. In order to find a working hydrant we had to go five or six blocks away. . . . At 2 A.M. on 9/12, we were relieved by others and were told to go home, get rest, and be ready to come back the next day. . . . What did I see? This was like nothing I could ever have imagined. There was 2–4 inches of concrete dust covering everything. Vehicles were upside-down, burned out FDNY vehicles were abandoned, glass was shattered everywhere, and buildings looked like they were bombed—like WWII photos in history books. There was paper flying all over the place and dark smoke still burning in parts of the rubble. Over the past three years I have developed friendships with some FDNY firemen. Some I have heard are safe, and some others I haven't heard from yet . . . pray for us all."

Thursday, September 13, 2001

"I slept about 3 hours after my last message. Unable to sleep, I started to get going but felt like a zombie. I did get some stuff done . . . God was in control. I ended up driving the van back to the city. By 1 P.M. I was back on top of the rubble assisting in

trying to reach victims. The lady next to me was looking into a hole—she stated that she thought someone was under this pile. We both then started to dig, and every time we moved another piece of rubble we would catch an odor of a victim. Others helped us dig, and after an hour we found a victim's foot. We continued to dig and exposed the victim up to the waist. But before we could finish, we were ordered to leave because a building was about to collapse. We had to leave this body where it was to save ourselves. Eventually they deemed that the building wasn't going to collapse, but another building was showing signs of collapse and they didn't want us near the area. . . . I am amazed at the number of people involved . . . police, fire, sheriffs from as far away as Liberty, PA—250 miles away. Salvation Army and other disaster services are giving out food and water . . . restaurants giving out all kinds of food and drinks . . . amazing how many people were working together for a common cause. Please keep up the prayers.

Saturday, September 15, 2001

Things have settled down around here. On Thursday the truck was sent home and we haven't been back to New York City since. It was good for me to get back to a normal routine . . . we may go out again . . . I don't know. Thanks for the prayers and emails this week. I was truly blessed. Continue to pray for members of the church and friends who are still working in the city.

Others in his church worked for months at Ground Zero after that September, as several members were either police or fire personnel.

Ken sees that God has worked in New York City in several specific ways. One, so many people feel blessed because they got out of the buildings or weren't there that day. Many more could have died or been injured. As pastor, Ken has worked with the families of some who died, bringing some to Christ and continuing to minister to others. God has used all kinds of people to bring help to a hurting metro area.

Ken and others he worked with saw things that were hard to forget during the days they worked "the pile." For believers like Ken, it is hope in Christ that helps us to get through these difficult times. Faith keeps us going when we feel we can't go on. Faith helps Ken continue being both pastor and firefighter—sometimes separately, sometimes together.

12

FIREFIGHTER RUSSELL STAMMER

Ten Firefighters Received Christ

When you first meet Russell Stammer, you notice his quiet spirit and jovial smile. His engaging personality makes you immediately feel comfortable around him. It is no big surprise to find out that this Toys "R" Us executive spends his free time fighting fires as a volunteer firefighter. Russ and his wife Eleanor have two children, Jonathan and Katie, and live in New Jersey, about 30 miles away from where the Twin Towers were. He and his wife are both Christians and attend their church faithfully, serving the Lord in whatever way they can. Russ is also president of the North Jersey chapter of the Fellowship of Christian Firefighters International. He and his colleagues feel it is important to reach out to other firefighters. Because of the stressful nature of the firefighter's life, Russell and others in the chapter use whatever ways they can to minister to firefighters. Firefighters who come to know Christ find they have a new perspective; their profession becomes more than just putting the fire out. They see it as a calling and a ministry, instead of just a job.

When the World Trade Center was hit, Russ was at work. He knew he might be called to go to the city, because they would be deploying fire personnel from the metro area eventually. This was big! He got the call, left work, went home and got some gear, and reported to the firehouse in Oakland, NJ. They were on standby until the end of the day, when they were told to stand down and go home. All the time he was waiting he remembered that only days earlier he and his family had been at the World Trade Center. How would he explain to his kids what had happened, and more than that, why it had happened?

Russell served as a fire chaplain at Liberty State Park in New Jersey, where they held a memorial service for victims' families. There, along with police chaplains and other fire chaplains, they presented urns of soil to about 300 families whose loved ones died in the attack. After the service, Russell was called to be an available chaplain for anyone who needed to talk. He wasn't sure what to say to the folks who would stop by, so he called out to God and asked for help. Here is an excerpt from an email he sent out.

Each family was escorted by a NJ state trooper. They were introduced to the acting governor of New Jersey, presented a flag by the NJ attorney general, and then escorted to one of four booths, where the chaplains made the presentations of the urns. Two chaplains handled the presentation. The families were then escorted out. As one woman came in, Patty (not her real name) stopped and said she wanted to talk to a chaplain. He looked at me as if to ask if I would talk with her. We spent about 20 or more minutes talking and praying together. She was doubting her faith and wondering if she could get through all this. I asked her if she believed in Jesus Christ, that He died on the cross for her sins, and that God created the heavens and earth. She stated that she did. I then said that she had more than enough faith to get through this. I reminded her that the Lord is with us and will provide us with whatever we need, including strength and faith, to get through anything that comes our way. We discussed that according to the Bible we only need faith the size of a mustard seed to have what we need. Once I felt that she had gotten the message she needed to hear, the Lord showed me a stuffed animal in a gift bag she was holding. It was a toy made by Russ Berrie, and the tag said RUSS on it. I asked her to read the label and asked her to do me a favor: whenever she started to doubt that she would have the faith and strength to get through, she should look at the tag and remember what Chaplain Russ had said about faith and the mustard seed.

Russ was honored that he had a glimpse into this family's world, honored that God allowed him to share God's love in this special moment.

Following the service, Russell went with another fire chaplain to Ground Zero and walked among the ruins. To fully describe the devastation is impossible. The smoke and fire exuded a smell that he will never forget. To see fire trucks and big city buses crushed was overwhelming. Concrete and debris were still all around the site, and remnants of the building were hovering, ready to fall.

Russell and the other chaplain tried to reach out to their firefighter brothers and sisters working there that day. They prayed for many and encouraged them to "keep on keeping on." They made sure firefighters were okay and found out what they needed. During the six hours they were there, ten firefighters received Christ. It was a moving time to see these big, grown men crying and hugging as they came into a relationship with Christ.

When Russ got home early the next morning, he told his wife that he wished she could have seen and experienced what he had. But at the same time, he was glad she had not. It took several days to get back to his old self. He kept thinking about what he had seen over and over again. He is grateful that he had seen and experienced the site so he could better pray for his colleagues in the city as they worked tirelessly every day.

Since 9-11, Russell and others in the Northern New Jersey Fellowship of Christian Firefighters have had continued opportunities to speak and to minister. In October 2002, Russ ministered at an official Fire Department of New York memorial at Madison Square Garden. He and hundreds of other Christian firefighters and volunteers made sure that they were there to encourage and care for the hurting families. Many people came to know the Lord that day. Once again, Russ saw the Lord using these opportunities to bring people to Him and find healing in Him.

Russ wants to continue to do whatever it takes to minister, especially to his brothers and sisters in the fire department. He feels an even deeper commitment to serve God. This event motivated Russ to be even more focused on the needs of firefighters and how the Fellowship can help them to know God in a more personal way.

Russ prays for two things out of this tragedy. One, that the church will see the importance of encouraging each other in service for the Lord, to "not give up meeting together, but to encourage each other all the more" (his paraphrase of Hebrews 10:25). His hope is that those who are Christian believers will also be more aware of those who serve them as firefighters. Fire personnel need a lot of encouragement to get through the difficult situations that they experience almost every day. Don't forget to stop by and encourage them and pray for them.

Russ also thinks of Jude 23, which says, "Snatch others from the fire and save them." As a firefighter, Russ feels that he is saving souls from literal fire. As a Christian firefighter, he is living out his faith to help others be saved from the eternal fire of separation from God.

FAITHFUL TO CARRY ON

13

PRINCIPAL ADA DOLCH

"Every Kid Is Safe"

Ada Dolch is principal at the High School for Leadership and Public Service in lower Manhattan. The school is located half a block from the old World Trade Center complex, now known as Ground Zero. Ada wants to be a testament to Jesus as she shepherds almost 600 students each day—with the help of great teachers and staff. The problems of adolescence stream through her office every day, and she depends on God to give her wisdom. Starting out her day with prayer and quiet helps her get ready to face whatever comes her way. She walks the halls praying over each classroom she passes.

Before September 11, Ada was given several words of encouragement through friends and fellow believers. Someone in her women's prayer group felt God wanted Ada to know that He would be using her in coming months to be a voice for Him. Her friend felt that she would be speaking to a lot of people about the Lord. Another person told her that she could see Ada speaking to the women of Wall Street (located blocks from her school). Not sure what this meant, Ada told the Lord she would do whatever came her way.

Ada and her teachers, staff, and students were only a few days into the new school year when September 11 came. Those words of encouragement others had given to her would soon be true. In her own words, here is her story of September 11 and the weeks and months that followed.

————

September 11 was primary election day in New York. People asked me later, "Did you feel strange that day? Did you fear something? Did you see something coming?" I said nope, I got up that day excited because our school would be a polling location for the first time. I got there by 5:45 A.M. to watch them set up. I was so excited that we, Public Service High, had arrived! We were expecting a mayoral candidate, Mike Bloomberg, to come by the school. I was thrilled to pieces.

Later that morning, I said to Lisa, my secretary, "The battery on my camera just died, so I'm going to run to the World Trade Center and get a battery." I took my walkie-talkie, my keys, and $5 in my pocket and went downstairs to the lobby, greeting the kids coming in as I normally do. I watched the election going on, people voting, a man reading a newspaper, a little old lady with two dogs, and an elderly couple running the election. It's funny, the things you remember. So I was watching and chitchatting, and the lights went out.

Day of Miracles

I refer to September 11 as the day of miracles. The first miracle was that I got caught up with the kids, got engaged in conversation, and didn't go to get my battery.

The second thing was that when the lights went out it forced me to be still—("Be still, and know that I am God," Psalm 46:10). I looked around, surveyed the situation, and watched, wanting to know where everything was. And then we heard that horrific sound—we knew it was an explosion.

I was standing in the lobby. School safety agents ran out—the police officer assigned to the election ran out. I looked out the window and could see the reflection of One World Trade, and I saw all this stuff spewing out of the building. Immediately I thought it might be an explosion, a bombing, another 1993 bomb. People were running into our building, screaming, crying, and trying to use their cell phones. One of my kids just entering the building said, "Mrs. Dolch, a plane hit that building." I thought, a Piper or a helicopter maybe, but a plane? A big plane? She said, "A big plane." A little boy came in, David, with tears streaming down his face, and he could not talk. I sat him down on a bench and asked, "David, tell me what's wrong." And he said, "A plane, a plane, a big plane, Mrs. Dolch, a big plane hit the building."

These kids had seen the plane hit, because they heard the plane as they were climbing the steps to school—the plane was so loud. I said, "Which building?" And David said, "The one with the antenna." I realized he was talking about the building where my sister works. I thought, "My God, my sister Wendy is up there!" I remember after the 1993 bombing we couldn't find my sister, either. So I said, "Lord, please take care of Wendy. I can't. I must take care of my kids. So she's in your hands." The next miracle is that I never thought of Wendy again. It was true amnesia. God just plucked her out of my brain. Later I found out that my sister had died.

I tried to make the appropriate phone calls, but the phones weren't working. The school's lobby became a command center and a place of refuge. People were running in the doors, in despair, crying hysterically, shaking. We found several tables and chairs for people to sit and calm themselves down. And then I began say, "We need Your peace, God. We need Your peace." He said, *Be still, and know that I am God.* I put my hands on people and prayed out loud, "The peace of God over you, Lord, the peace that surpasses all understanding." And then I thought, oh my, I'm speaking out loud, I'm in school— and then I thought, who cares! I remember saying things like that.

At the same time, I positioned people in the building. At that time, only Tower One had been hit. We thought everything was over. Lisa said, "Your husband called. Your sister from New Jersey called, and I told them we're all okay."

Then the second plane hit. And it was total chaos. Our building shook. By then, I knew where the kids were. I had wanted the kids to stay in their classrooms, but then the second plane hit, and it became bedlam in the lobby. It was truly a sea of people. We were hearing, "It's terrorism." I was thinking, We're right next door to the American Stock Exchange. We're across the street from Trinity Church. People were coming into the building, and I didn't know who they were. What if there's a terrorist trying to come into this building to hurt the kids? I was praying over people, and I was going, Okay Lord, now what? I surveyed the situation. I had some girls in wheelchairs taken to the lobby. I had a blind girl, and a girl who just had heart surgery. I needed to get them out of there while the power was still working. It was a miracle that I was making decisions and functioning—I couldn't even figure out what was going on. In retrospect, I thought, Where did that come from? Well, where else—the Lord!

So I thought, We've all got to leave. If someone's trying to hurt us, I've got to get us out of here. Tower Two is right here; we're going to catch on fire. I was frantic! So I stood up on a table and said, "I am the principal of this school. My name is Ada Dolch. I am the principal. I must have everyone's attention."

Silence came all of a sudden.

So I thought, Okay, so what am I going to tell them? "We're evacuating the building. We're going south to Battery Park. You must leave now." It was like I was a crazy woman. Everyone was following my directions. I spoke to the assistant principal on the walkie-talkie—go floor to floor all the way to the top, make sure everyone is out! We were constantly making announcements on the speaker system so everyone would know what was going on.

Evacuating the School

I stood outside as each kid came out. I greeted them; I touched them. The kids that I know are faith-believing children, I told them this is the time to be praying. Grab a neighbor, stay together, until we all got out. My assistant principal was the last one out with my secretaries and some other teachers. As far as we could tell, there was no one left in the building. So I looked at the custodian and told him, "The building is yours, good luck." We all started to walk down to Battery Park.

When we had gone about three blocks, I looked up for the first time. And I saw what you saw on television—the two towers aflame. And I said to my assistant principal, "Ted, do you see what I see?" People kept coming to us for information because we had those walkie-talkies, and I kept saying, "We're not sure, but we need to get far away from here because it's not safe. So let's move in that direction. Everybody, come on, we've got to go to the park." People followed us because we looked official; little did they know we were just a bunch of teachers and kids making their way like everyone else!

As we got to the park entrance, I stopped the traffic, got all the kids across, and then we heard the noise I will never forget. I looked back, and there was a cloud as high as the buildings. It was coming toward us. We ran because we didn't know what was coming in that cloud. The kids and people in the park were now scattered and screaming and running; I was pushed three different times. I was wearing heels and a long skirt, and couldn't run. And just as it was about to hit us, I looked around and thought, If I'm going to die, I'm not going to die in the middle of the street.

The Cloud

I found a tree with a bench and a fence behind it and got beside it, on the ground. There were other Christians there, on their knees, screaming out to the Lord, and so I joined in. Then the cloud hit. It didn't knock us over, but it pulled us along. I put my head down, in case there was something hard in the cloud. It was black, pitch black. Couldn't see a thing. I just screamed through it, "MERCY, FATHER, MERCY! You said You wouldn't leave us or forsake us."

Just as quick as the darkness came, that's how fast it went. The momentum was so intense that it dissipated just as quickly. It went from black to gray to light gray to white ash. I realized I couldn't pray anymore—I couldn't swallow. It was as if there were knives cutting into my throat; I could feel it on my skin. It was itchy—it hurt. I couldn't swallow. There was a water fountain nearby, and a man with his finger holding the spigot for others, and people were taking water and spitting. And I thought, Water in the park, that is a miracle! The man had torn off a piece of his jacket, gotten it wet, and put it over his mouth. And he was telling people, "You have to spit, you have to spit." I was going, "I'm a principal—I don't spit." And I realized I couldn't swallow it. You had to spit and clear your throat. Men were cutting up their jackets and their shirts and giving them to people to wet and put over their faces.

I had tissues—why did I have tissues? Because when the second plane hit, my secretary jumped out of her seat, ran into my office, and thought, What will Ada need? She got my pocketbook. There I was, in Battery Park with my pocketbook. Pretty cool. So I wet the tissues and put them over my mouth. My eyes were burning. I tried to wipe the stuff off my face.

Then I looked around, thinking, Where are my kids? Lord, just take care of them, wherever they are, just take care of them. We started walking, praying, and were trying to find kids through the radio. I saw people getting on the ferries. I saw some of my teachers lined up against a wall. Then the second building collapsed, and a cloud hit us again. It wasn't as intense as the first time—I don't know why. I think the first time it hit us straight on, and the second time it went off into the water. Again I was on the ground pleading for mercy. And I began to find people with the walkie-talkie, and I remember saying goodbye to kids, saying, "Be good! Behave!" I didn't know where they were going. No idea.

Then I saw the American Café restaurant, which I never knew existed before that day. Inside were about 200 of my kids, cutting up the tablecloths, wetting them, and giving them to people. Management had opened the back kitchens, and people were going back and washing themselves. The kids were somber, and they were all saying, "What just happened?" They started asking me some questions—I don't even remember what they were asking me. Kenisha said, "Mrs. Dolch, you have to wash your face. And you really need lipstick."

I said, "Thanks Kenisha, I'll put it right on." I had my pocketbook! So I went into the kitchen and splashed my face. When I came out, a worker was allowing people to use the telephone, which had started working. I was standing next to him, so I was the second person to use the phone. Positioning—all about positioning. I called the superintendent and told him, "Every kid is out—no one is in the building! I can't tell you where they all are, but we all walked out together. We went to Battery Park. Some have gone on the ferries; there are about 200 in my possession. You must promise to call my husband and tell him that I am okay."

I walked outside with the kids, we sat, and we talked. I saw my girls in the wheelchairs—we were finding a lot of the kids. There were helicopters flying overhead, and we didn't know if they were ours, or the enemy trying to get us again. I don't remember this at all, but my secretary tells me there was a young boy having a very bad asthma attack, and I said, "Let's lay hands on him and pray." His breathing calmed down and he was able to get a handle on things.

An hour or two after it began, we came up with a plan to get people home. We broke people up into sections with teachers to lead them home, because there was no reason to stay there. People showed up from nowhere giving out bottles of water—boxes and boxes of water. People were giving out masks. I also remember distinctly the sirens, nonstop, like turning it on and never hearing it go off.

The Little Muslim Girl

I took the group going up to Brooklyn. There must have been 30–40 people following me. We went to the Brooklyn Bridge, but it was closed—too many people. We kept walking north, to the Manhattan Bridge. As we crossed that bridge, a little Muslim girl wearing a head covering walked next to me and said, "Mrs. Dolch, I'm so afraid, I'm so afraid, I'm scared." And I said, "What are you afraid of? Look, we're crossing the bridge. The sun is shining; it's warm, it feels wonderful. Come, let's sing a song." I don't remember what we were singing.

In retrospect, I see that this was an angel in the form of a little Muslim girl. Why did we meet each other? Because I developed such a relationship with her that not for one second could I harbor hatred toward Muslim people. That was one of the most poignant moments and a turning point in my life. I couldn't do it. I love this little girl. She always says, "Mrs. Dolch, I love you so much."

Later, this little girl came to school without her head covering. I asked her where it was. She said, "Whatever I am—I can hold in my heart." So I look at her with a smile. I've told her how God used her to protect me from ever being angry or hating Muslim people.

Every Kid Is Safe

So on to Brooklyn. I got to the Board of Education, and I literally fell onto the steps—it dawned on me what I had been through. I began to cry. I walked up the steps; I tried to explain to them who I am. They brought me in to the chancellor; I started to cry and said, "Chancellor, every kid is safe. We evacuated that building—there isn't one kid you have to worry about." He was shaking—you can't imagine. Couldn't give me his box of tissues he was shaking so much.

I believe that I became his angel—I was able to tell him that all the kids were safe. Which meant all the kids were safe—every kid in New York City was safe. Because not one kid in New York City perished—not one kid.

God turns all evil for good. The Bible has become a living document in my life. If I never saw it again, it's a living document. It just bubbles. A truly bubbling fountain—it's so real. That's the most incredible thing when I think about this horrific tragedy, this heinous attack. And all it's done is brought me closer to Jesus, not farther away. My shelter, my refuge, my fortress. And when I walk through the valley of the shadow of death, I just smell the lilies. He is the lily of the valley. I smell the lilies, and I know He's there.

Let's be real—I've had some very difficult moments. Some very hard moments. I lost my sister. We had a memorial service. God is my strength. I don't know what else to say. There were times when I wondered how I am doing this. Times when I cried for two days straight. But I never lost my hope or my faith. The flesh is real, the flesh hurts.

But the greatest thing has happened—I have been asked to speak in so many places. I've become a voice—

His voice, to say there is an answer, you can find refuge only in Him. He is my strength—no matter where I speak or what the venue is, that's the message I declare. Because of the publicity, I've developed this little relationship with Alan Houston of the Knicks. He had been a keynote speaker at graduation two years before. He is a Christian. Praise God for him!

Every year, Fortune 500 has a conference on Wall Street for Fortune 500 women. After September 11, a woman called me and invited me to speak at this conference. I thought I would fall on the floor! I asked, "What do you want me to speak about?" She said, "You have five minutes—tell your story and relate it to leadership. And remember, you're speaking to a group of powerful women. What message do you want to leave behind for powerful women?"

So I sat at the computer for two days and planned how I would tell them my story. When I was a little girl in Sunday school, we memorized Psalm 23, so I started with Psalm 23, and I told them the story.

I spoke to these women about strength and power—these are powerful women. I spoke of leadership—Jesus is my leader. These women know about having a mission, having a vision—so I spoke about knowing what your mission in life is and using your position to accomplish that mission. Life is not about money, and you know that. What role are you going to play in the future, in children's lives? What are you going to contribute on their journey?

I ended my speech and looked into the audience—they were cheering, standing, clapping. I couldn't believe it. I prayed, "Oh God, get me off this stage." But I remembered that my friend had told me God was going to give me this opportunity.

There were dark moments when I would say, God where are you? And I would get on the Internet and find an email message with a word from God, a Scripture verse. These came from people I didn't know—Catholic, Pentecostal, and Baptist people were very encouraging.

Life was strange for a long time. We had to borrow space at an uptown school until our building was cleaned and the streets were opened. It was hard on the students and the teachers. But thank God we were only displaced for 4 months. The wonder of it all is that we got to the other side. You've got to stand strong and you will get to the other side!

Here's my testimony: Hope is only in God—there is nothing else but Him. It's so simple, but we make it so difficult. God is truly the fortress in the most difficult moments. He lifts us up when we're in the deepest valley. He's like the eagle, and we just get on those wings, and He lifts us way up. To have faith is to have seen the end. To have faith is to be able to say I know what the end of the book is. No matter what comes before me, because of what I've chosen to believe, and the One I derive my strength from, I know that there's a good end to the story.

14

FREEMAN FIELD

Terror Through a Classroom Window

The terrorist attacks of September 11 took a toll on the whole city of New York, but one group that didn't get much attention was that of the schools around Ground Zero. Many students attended school at alternative sites for up to 6 months, and much of their year was full of chaos. Freeman Field attended Stuyvesant High School, located 2 blocks north of the World Trade Center. On September 11, he was about a week into his senior year of high school. He had been chosen as captain of his school's football team, and he was looking at colleges to attend after graduation. On the day of the attacks, he had a full view of the terror. Freeman had looked forward to a great year, but he and other students instead found their senior year contaminated by the horror of the attacks. Below, Freeman shares what he remembers of the day and how he sees that God worked in the midst of a terrible situation.

I had just gotten to science class, my first class of the day. The classroom is on the 7th floor and has a window facing the World Trade Center. Everyone was looking down the street because they heard this loud bang. We thought that there was a car crash or something. We saw people running around, but we couldn't see what was going on. So we lost interest after a while and sat down.

Then an announcement was made on the loudspeaker that a plane had crashed into the World Trade Center. We saw this huge cloud of smoke coming from that direction. We turned on the television to watch the live coverage. Some people were looking out the window again and saw the second plane hit. As soon as it hit, we saw this huge ball of fire come out of the building. Just crazy.

After that everyone was kind of hysterical—everyone, including our teacher, was crying. They came on the loudspeaker again and told us to go about our day as if it were normal, as if we just had regular classes. We couldn't believe it! We were like, this is ridiculous, a plane just hit the World Trade Center, and we're supposed to go on as if nothing has happened. But we all went on to our next class. I went to my history class, on the second floor, also facing the WTC. Our teacher was helping other kids make phone calls to make sure their parents were okay—people who might have been in the WTC. We looked out and saw the lights flicker and heard this loud crash, and we saw the first tower crash and a huge cloud of smoke coming toward our building. The teachers were yelling, "Get away from the window!" So we did. Everything was okay, and the cloud didn't come up to the school.

They came on the loudspeaker again and told us to go to our homeroom, which would be our normal class, and to go about as a normal day. Again, this was ridiculous! So my friend Paul, who lived just next to the WTC, and I decided to meet downstairs to make a phone call to see if his family was okay. There was a huge line for the pay phones, but everyone was okay in his family.

Evacuating the School

We started to go into the school's theater, where they said we could stay if we wanted to. But as we were going into the auditorium, teachers started pushing us out the door, saying, "They're evacuating the school, they're evacuating the school!" They started sending us out the north exit, the side away from the WTC. So we started going out and walking up the West Side Highways, and we heard another large crash, so we turned around and saw the 2nd tower going down. We saw a cloud of smoke and debris coming toward us, and everyone started running. We were running from the cloud, and we kept running until we felt we had escaped it! We got to a safe distance and stopped to make sure all our friends were okay.

My friends lived in Brooklyn, Queens, Bronx, and Staten Island (our high school brings kids from all over the city). But they couldn't go home, because the subways were shut down. My house is about a mile away from school, so they all came home with me and waited it out until the transit system came back on line and everything was okay. There were about 14 of us, and we gathered around the TV and watched what we could since the networks were down—the TV towers had been on top of the WTC. It was bizarre—like something out of a movie. It was crazy.

It was strange in the weeks afterwards. To know that my friend lives right there. It was just weird to think— like, when we walked to his house, we'd walk through the WTC, to the train station. We walked there almost every weekend. Now, it's just gone! Nothing seemed the same. Looked like a war zone!

Our football team decided we needed to do something. The coach had emailed all of us and told us we were meeting at Chelsea Piers, the headquarters of where they were donating stuff. So we went there, but they didn't need any volunteers. So they sent us to the Salvation Army, where they needed volunteers to load up trucks to drive down to Ground Zero. We spent a Saturday down there loading trucks. While we were at Chelsea Piers, they were taking names for Chefs with Spirit, sponsored by Chef Cruises. It was a ship that was right by Ground Zero where relief workers could come and get a hot meal. And we went down and served them, from 6 P.M. to 6 A.M. It was really good—a bunch of the seniors and I signed up and did it. It was good. It was a little weird, though, because this was their time to relax and get everything out of their minds. Everyone was really happy to be there. But there were some that were just depressed. And one guy had found too many dead bodies, like a body of a guy, just his shoulders and above, with his jacket on. He just couldn't believe the things he was seeing. It was horrible to them!

Since we didn't have school for a few weeks, I was mostly at home during that time; it was weird to think about what was going on. Besides volunteering, I didn't really leave the house much that week. It just made me think about what happened. It really gave me time to reflect on what happened, and the effects. I had time just to reflect and talk to my parents about it, have quiet time with God about it. I could really try and get back to normal, like the way it was before the WTC happened.

Back to Normal?

Will we ever get back to normal? I think for the most part, yes. It's still weird, when we go to my friend's house, to take the long way around and not just walk through. For a while, we had to go to Brooklyn to go to school at another building, but since having gotten back, you look down the block and there's this huge gaping hole in the street. Other than that, I think everything kind of went back to normal. It's senior year, so everyone's back in that mindset, doing what they would do their senior year! We are trying to make up for the loss that we had those first few weeks!

As I think about how I am coping, I think you have to find the balance between talking about it and going back to normal. Talking about it is really important, just to sort it out. But when you get to the point where you're dwelling on it, it becomes too much. That's why you just try to do the things you would do normally. Go out, go see a movie, do something that you would do if it hadn't happened. But don't just hold it all in. It will all bottle up and come out when you don't want it to. It's unhealthy to bottle it all up.

I pray and ask God to help me and my friends to deal with this because I believe that will be the best way to heal . . . through God! Mostly when I think about it I just take some deep breaths to calm myself down. I think that God knows what to do to help people. The Bible does say that good things can come from bad situations. As horrible as this all is, it might not balance out, but God always has a plan. It's all in His plan—you'll find out what His plan was eventually.

It is exciting to me to think that everyone has kind of bonded together as a community—in New York, especially. There's such unity within New York, I think. People have been nicer to each other, not just flipping you off for everything like they used to. I also think it's created some really good opportunities to share your faith with people. Events like this just get you thinking about life after death and the existence of God. It's an open door to share your faith with other people.

I think all the prayer has been comforting to everyone—helping out and being with people and calling on God to be with people. Since we have that relationship with God, we should just use it to get through this hard time.

— · —

Freeman graduated from high school and is a student at Baylor University in Waco, Texas. His graduation was a tender time for all of his classmates and teachers as they remembered what had happened in the fall. Time does heal, and as we move forward in life, we heal and the pain gets a little less. Freeman has a personal relationship with Jesus Christ to help him in the future as memories of 9-11 come back. He knows that he can call on God to be with him in the hard times and good times. Jesus is alive and is growing Freeman to be a man who can help others in pain. God will use his experience to minister to many others in the future!

15

OWEN FIELD

"God Can Mend the Scars"

Owen Field couldn't be called an "average" 17-year-old. He is quite bright and has a gentle, vibrant personality. Everyone remembers Owen when they meet him; he has the ability to make a caring impression on others. He has been writing songs and playing guitar for quite a while and is a part of the praise band at his church, East Seventh Baptist Church in lower Manhattan. He seems to be very much in tune with Christ, and his intuitive side causes him to sometimes blurt out thoughts that are pretty deep for someone his age.

Owen has a number of good, solid friends and has been known on occasion to have a good tussle with his brother Freeman, who is about 2 years older. Owen excels in school and attends a top high school in New York City, Bronx High School for Science and Math. Unlike teenagers in most parts of the U.S., Owen takes a subway through two boroughs to get to school.

On September 11, Owen woke up and went through his morning routine to get to school. As he was sitting in his classroom waiting for class to begin, he heard on his

Walkman that airplanes had hit the World Trade Center. Owen told the class what he was hearing, and then others in class began to hear the same thing. Rumors were flying, and the radio announcers were throwing all sorts of information out over the airwaves.

Some of Owen's friends began to panic—especially kids whose parents worked at the World Trade Center or who had firefighter dads. Students and teachers were wondering what to do as they tried to get in touch with loved ones. Owen remembers that people were crying and upset, and that everybody seemed to be running for the phones.

In all the chaos, although he was nervous and anxious, Owen felt a peace he had not felt before. One friend even commented that he was impressed that Owen trusted God so easily. Owen was concerned, though, because his brother Freeman attended school two blocks away from the trade center. As the towers fell, he hoped and prayed that his brother was okay. He was able to leave not too long afterward to go home, although his familiar route—the subway from school to his home in lower Manhattan—was blocked. Train service had shut down completely. He took a cab as far as the bridge that crosses Manhattan and walked across. After getting to Manhattan, he took a cab as far south as 33rd Street and walked the rest of the way home to find his brother, safe and sound, with a few of his friends gathered around the TV watching the scenes unfold. It was mind-boggling that this could happen so close to his home (Owen's home is about a mile from the WTC). They spent the rest of the day close to the TV. Owen was amazed that he could feel God's peace in the midst of such chaos.

The next morning he got up and went for a run along the East River as he always did. As he ran farther south, he felt that things were getting really eerie. Smoke poured out still from the site, and a haze hung heavy over the island. As Owen got to closer to the site, smoke and dust filled the air, making it difficult to keep running. He decided to stop and turned to go back home. As he made his way back uptown, he saw police cars that had been crushed by the debris, and some police officers resting at places along the way. Not many people were out that day, so it made the surroundings even more dream-like.

Many things over the next months would be dream-like and surreal. Those months were fragile times; some of his classmates were having a hard time dealing with the death and destruction that had come their way. The teenage years are already a tumultuous time, and this tragedy added to the turmoil. Owen chose to draw near to God during this time, and as he did, he began to heal. As he had opportunity, he shared that with friends.

One way he dealt with his feelings was to use his musical talent to write a song about the day.

Ordinary Day
by Owen Field

Just an ordinary day, people worked away
    in an office just like any other day.
Flying machines that lost their way
    turned the world to disarray,
In a haze of blue and gray on the ordinary day.

Chorus
Torn apart,
    only God can mend the scars on our heart,
    they will never fade away.
Towers fell down and we looked to the sky
    to the One who knows the reasons why
    it all came crashing down.
Peace could not be found.

We try not to tell of it
    because life is just too delicate.
Visions flood our minds we can't forget.
Death was a price some did pay,
    buried where their killers lay,
Tomorrow is another ordinary day.

Chorus
Torn apart,
    only God can mend the scars on our heart
    that will never fade away.
Towers fell down and we looked to the sky
    to the One who knows the reasons why
    it all came crashing down.
Peace could not be found.

Owen has sung that song several times in public and even recorded it for a CD at his church. He has seen his own heart being healed as he has allowed Christ to come into his life more than before. This 17-year-old has learned that no problem is bigger than God; it is rare for someone his age to really know that truth. He believes that, no matter what, God will help you. If you die and know Him, you can't lose. If you live, this is a chance for you to give all your worries to Him and let Him take care of you. But, as Owen says, you have to give your worries to Him or He can't help you. Owen has seen his love for God intensify over the last year and a half.

The future holds a lot for Owen as he gets older and makes life decisions. He is a musician and is also interested in business. He knows that this event in his life will be in his memory for as long as he lives. It will not be just another story out of a history book that his children and grandchildren will read. He will be able to tell them what happened from his own experience and how God loved him and others. Owen knows that as he grows in his own journey with Christ, he will continue to see that "in all things God works for the good of those who love him, who have been called according to his purpose" (Romans 8:28). Even when you have pain in your life, you can know a peace that goes beyond your own understanding.

16

NORM JONES

Escape from Tower Two

Norm Jones, a member of Plymouth Church in Brooklyn, New York, is an accountant who worked in Tower Two of the World Trade Center. Norm feels he made it home the day of September 11 only by the strength and grace of God. He kept a journal of the event so he wouldn't forget that day. Many people died a horrific death. Norm not only had to deal with the death of colleagues and business acquaintances, but also the shock of what happened that day. It hasn't been easy, but with God to help him along the way, Norm knows he is not alone.

Norm is like many Christians in the way he came to have a relationship with Christ. Growing up in Pennsylvania, he went to church and Sunday School, read the Bible, and was involved in church. Around the age of 12, he publicly confirmed his faith in Christ. Norm says that "from then on, I never had a doubt that God was going to be with me all the time." God gave him the gift of trust that would prove to be unshakable throughout his life. That faith has taken him through school, marriage, career, and now a family.

This faith helped a strong, peaceful man get through one of the hardest days of his life on September 11, 2001. Norm had no doubt that God helped him, and that God was all around on that day. Norm truly felt the strength and courage that only an unshakable faith could give. Here is his story in his own words.

——

On the morning of Tuesday, September 11, I arrived a little early at my office on the 71st floor of Tower Two of the World Trade Center to make sure that some electronic data files had been emailed to an affiliated company in Chicago. Of the 200 people who worked on my floor, about 20 people had arrived that day. My colleague Tom was in his office next to mine. The mailroom guys were making their early morning rounds, delivering reports for the day. A few other people were getting an early start to the day.

Then it happened. I didn't know what time it was, but the newspaper said it was 8:45 A.M. There was a loud noise from One World Trade Center, the North Tower. Our tower, the South Tower, shook. My office faced away from the North Tower, so I didn't see it happen. But I did see a brief ball of flame around my side of the building, followed by a blizzard of paper, like a ticker-tape parade.

We didn't know what had happened. I assumed some kind of electrical equipment had exploded on the upper floors of the other tower. I heard a curse from next door. Tom and I both got up to see what was going on. We were both veterans on the '93 World Trade Center bombing, so we were still calm.

Patrick, another manager and also our floor safety captain, went to the special red emergency phone in the lobby of our floor to find out what was happening and what we should do. He said there were so many people yelling on the phone at the same time that he couldn't find out anything.

I immediately called Jacque, my wife. I told her something had happened in Tower One but not to worry, our tower was fine. As a spouse, she was also a veteran of the '93 bombing, but I wanted to make sure she wasn't alarmed.

An announcement came over the emergency system, which was added after the last bombing. I don't remember the exact words, but it was something to the effect that there had been an incident in Tower One but there was no need to evacuate our tower at the present time, as Tower Two was secure. I remembered thinking how calm and professional the announcer sounded. I wondered if he had special voice training in order to project calmness in case of panic. If so, he was an A student.

We believed the announcement. We knew there would be chaos downstairs from the evacuation of Tower One. It seemed to be smarter and more efficient to let them evacuate first, then we could evacuate later when we had more information and could avoid the crowds and confusion. We're cool-headed, logical accountants—what can I say?

The situation quickly deteriorated. The people on our floor whose offices faced the North Tower started yelling that Tower One was on fire and people were starting to break the windows and jump out. Some watched in sickly horror and fascination. I avoided the sight. I did not want those images to haunt me the rest of my life.

Then came another announcement: "There is no immediate danger, but you may evacuate the building if you wish."

I quickly called Jacque again. "Tower One is on fire and people are jumping out of the building. But our building is fine. Don't worry." Those were meant to be reassuring words to my wife. I guess I wasn't as calm and as rational as I thought. That was the last she was to hear from me for the next hour and half.

The few remaining people on the floor decided it was time to get out. I picked up my bag and copied the spreadsheet I was working on onto a disk. After all, there was a chance we might not be able to get back into the building for a while. Tom was making a last-minute call before walking out. We headed for the central corridor stairwells to start making our evacuation. Tom had forgotten something and started back to his office to pick it up. "Forget your @#$% bag," Patrick said.

Then it happened again. Our building shook to its timbers. Somebody said they saw flames. There was an odd smell. The ceiling tiles in the central corridor started collapsing around us. This was the last sign we needed— we were out of there. We checked the nearest stairwell— much better than in '93 when we had to walk down in pitch darkness. Some of the walls in the stairwell were seriously cracked, but otherwise all seemed well. By this time the stairways were uncrowded.

There was no panic. People were making feeble jokes to relieve tension. I mentioned how lucky we were that this happened on a dress-down day so we wouldn't get our suits dirty.

Around the 64th floor, we caught up with two women slowly working their way down the stairs. One was apparently on crutches; the other was holding the crutches, trying to help her. What to do? We paused briefly. Tom and I got on either side of her, and we tried to pick her up by both arms, but that didn't work at all. Tom then lifted her up and threw her over his shoulders and started down. Six floors later he needed a break, so it was my turn for six floors. Soon it was one floor for Tom, then one for me. It was pretty slow going. Her friend with the crutches had gone on ahead. Our evacuee was worried about where her crutches were, but we weren't.

Then, thank God, around the 44th floor, another Good Samaritan came along, named Louis. He hoisted the woman over his shoulder and managed to carry her the remaining 40-plus floors by himself.

Our descent was steady again, although slow. Louis was starting to get hot. Someone whipped out a bottle of water and poured it over his head. The journey continued. Further down we caught up with one of our senior portfolio managers, who was winded and had stopped for a rest. Louis and his party continued ahead. I continued slowly with the portfolio manager. Other stragglers, including a pregnant woman, were still working their way down, each with their Good Samaritans accompanying them.

At last the emergency stairwell dumped us out onto the mezzanine level of our tower. We could see a little real daylight ahead for the first time in many minutes. The hall was normally used by tourists coming from the observation deck of our tower. The hallways were filled with bright, glitzy ads for Broadway shows—somewhat incongruous after our journey. A policewoman was there directing us to go further down the hall to an exit.

Finally we were in total daylight on the mezzanine level. We could see rubble everywhere on the plaza. On the huge lobby of our tower, we saw a couple hundred firemen lining up in front of the elevator to begin a search and rescue mission through the building. We knew by this time we were almost certain to get out. But what about these brave firemen? What must have been going through their minds, knowing that they were getting ready to go up into a building that every sensible person was now evacuating? I will always have the greatest respect for their bravery and their courage.

At last we were out on the street. The portfolio manager and I shook hands—we had really made it out. We crossed the street and merged into the milling throng and then went our separate ways. I had lost everyone else in our vagabond group coming down. I turned around and took my first look at Tower One. The top floors were all in flames. At last the enormity of the disaster started to sink in.

I continued down the street. I ran into one of our accountants and assured him that I would see him in our disaster recovery center in Jersey City later in the day. Fortunately, he paid no attention to me. Then I came across a secretary from Morgan Stanley's World Trade Center facilities department. After the 1993 bombing, she was the Dean Witter czar; she determined who got the coveted building passes that would allow ten people back into the tower to recover business and computer files in the weeks after the bombing. I asked her if she was prepared to start this process all over again. She just took another drag on her cigarette, and I walked on.

Now that I was free, the only thing I wanted to do was get to a phone and call Jacque. Cell phones weren't working because the streets were mobbed with people. Pay phones in this area rarely worked on a good day. In my daze, I thought of some friends, Alan and Linda, who lived on the other side of downtown Manhattan. Maybe their housekeeper would be home and let me in.

I rang their doorbell and tried to explain through the intercom that I was Chris and Angela's dad. "Remember me from when I picked them up from play dates? Could I come in?" Linda was home that day, and she immediately invited me up and had a cold glass of water ready. I asked to use the phone.

I called Jacque and told her I was okay. She heaved a big sigh of relief. I had no idea that her office had been following the minute-by-minute updates on the Internet and also TV. She has her own stories to tell about working at her school, Packer Collegiate, to get her kids and their families back together after the disaster. Our kids were also at the school, going through their own anxiety.

Then I called my parents. My mother answered and was ecstatic to hear my voice. Their prayers had been answered. I didn't have much else to say at this point except that I was okay and as far as I knew everyone on my floor must have been okay.

Linda was watching the news on TV while I was on the phone. I heard her gasp that one of the towers had collapsed. This couldn't be! The World Trade Center buildings could never collapse. They were too strong. They had easily withstood the bombing in '93. At this point I was too stunned to react. The news ticker at the bottom of the TV screen said that President Bush promised a full investigation.

A little later, Chris, my oldest son, called. He was glad to know that I was alive. But then he said his friend

Nick's dad worked on the 100th floor of Tower One. He asked if I thought Nick's dad got out okay. I didn't know what to say. I knew there wasn't a prayer that anyone that high in Tower One was alive. For the first time, tears came down my face. Fortunately, I found out later that Nick's dad had stopped to vote on the way to work—it was primary day in New York City. So Nick's dad was not in the building when it came down.

By now there was a steady stream of people on the street outside the apartment, making their way to homes on the other side of Brooklyn. They looked like refugees, except these people were better-dressed.

Linda and her neighbors began distributing drinking water and rags to use as face masks to the people passing by. I couldn't stand to watch TV anymore, so I helped Linda and her housekeeper cut up old bed sheets to hand out. Most were grateful for the water and the rags. Linda and her neighbor had quite an operation going.

After a while I decided it was time to get home. I said my thanks to Linda and joined in the mass exodus across the Brooklyn Bridge. There were no cars on the bridge, just an occasional emergency vehicle rushing by. The bridge was wall-to-wall with pedestrians. I couldn't help thinking as I crossed the bridge that if terrorists could fly two planes into the World Trade Center, they could just as easily fly another into the Brooklyn Bridge. I didn't feel comfortable until my feet were on solid ground on the other side.

I was back in my home neighborhood. The first land-mark I passed was a local neighborhood bakery and deli. I stopped to buy a bottle of water. I saw the owner and joked with him that it was becoming a tradition for me to buy water there after every World Trade Center bombing. (I had done the same thing in 1993.) I don't think he got the joke.

The second neighborhood landmark was our church, Plymouth Church of the Pilgrims. I stopped by to tell anyone who was there that I was okay. The church music director rushed in and embraced me like a lost brother. The senior minister, the president of the church council, and the chair of the membership committee were organizing the church's response to the disaster. Hastily they threw open the church doors and provided a small prayer service for anyone who walked by.

As I approached my apartment building, the building superintendent ran up and embraced me. He had been trying to find out about me. I thanked him and headed upstairs. Our housekeeper, Lydia, gave me the biggest Polish hug I have ever had in my life. She had watched my tower collapse from the Brooklyn Heights promenade, which overlooked downtown Manhattan, and thought I must be dead. She had frantically been trying to keep in touch with Jacque to get any news. "How could this happen in America?" she asked. This was the land of safety and freedom.

As it turns out, we got to repay Linda for the favor she had done me. Our children attend school together, and their kids spent that night at our house. Alan and Linda were without water and electricity for the remainder of the week. Alan was stranded in Phoenix, Arizona, and couldn't get home. So Linda and her two kids, Jeremy and Gavin, moved in with us for a few days. We tried to make it like a giant sleepover party for our kids, so they wouldn't focus on the anguish going on around us. In the following days, I was to resume work at our backup site across the river in Jersey City, New Jersey.

Norm has continued to rely on his faith as he moves forward and goes about his daily life. He knows that God is in charge and that even as other challenges come his way, he can face them with God's strength. Norm proved that verse in Scripture that says, "I can do everything through him who gives me strength" (Philippians 4:13).

17

ANNETTE LEGG

"God, Protect My Baby"

Annette Legg was almost eight months pregnant in September of 2001, and the pregnancy had been a challenging one. She traveled an hour every day from her Orange County, New York, home to her job at the Marriott Hotels. She worked in the sales office for the Financial Centers and World Trade Center Marriott Hotels. Her office was located in the Financial Center Hotel, about a block and a half south of the WTC complex. Here is her account of that day.

———

On September 11, 2001, I was almost 8 months pregnant (31 weeks, to be exact). That morning, I took the train to work as usual. I got off the train at the World Trade Center Tower Two exit and crossed Liberty Street to walk the short distance to my office at the hotel. I remember thinking it was such a gorgeous day. The people from the farmer's market were setting up, and it was beautiful outside. I planned to leave work at noon that day so I could be on time to the open house at my son's school that night. That morning, my daughter asked me, "Mommy, can I go to work with you?" I remember thinking for a minute that maybe she could, but I explained to her that I would be home early and would spend time with her that afternoon.

I had gestational diabetes during all my pregnancies, a condition that would disappear after delivery. With this pregnancy, I tested my blood seven times a day and took four daily insulin shots. I had to eat breakfast because of my morning insulin shot. My habit was to inject myself upon arrival at work, wait about 15 minutes, and then order out for breakfast.

On 9-11, I had just ordered breakfast for my boss, a coworker, and myself when the first plane hit. Our lights flickered, and we felt a tremble in our building. We joked about the tremble being related to the construction going on in our building. At the rear of our office, a coworker was looking out the window and he said, "No guys, I think it's more than just construction." We looked and saw papers flying, little bundles of wires on fire scattered on the sidewalks below, and we immediately heard the sirens.

I Doubted It Was Terrorism

We left the office immediately. On our way down, some- one told us a small plane had hit one of the towers. We walked out through the back of the hotel and could not believe what was happening. Cars were moving and people were still in the streets below. We had a clear view of the towers. One of my coworkers immediately turned to me and said, "This is no accident, this is terror- ism." I remember thinking, "Oh my God, this is awful," but I doubted it was terrorism. My sister Valerie worked in Tower Two, on the 22nd floor. I knew my mother would see the news and panic. I had kidded with my sister when she took the job, "Don't worry about it—if anything happens, you're only 22 floors up." Little did I know.

As we saw the chaotic streets, I remember saying, "God bless those people," offering up a prayer because I knew there would be casualties, although I never expected as many as there were. Allison, a coworker who was also pregnant, walked up, crying. She had been outside when it happened, and ran through the falling debris. We took her to our restaurant to calm her down. She had stopped at a café to pick up an egg sandwich and still had it in her hands.

I needed to call my mother and my husband, but the phone in the restaurant wasn't working. Without thinking, I took the elevator to the second floor (I thought later how crazy I was to get into the elevator). There were only a few people in our office, and the phones were ringing off the hook. I called my sister's office first and got no answer—I was sure they had vacated their offices. I called my mother and left a message telling her not to worry, that Valerie had most likely left her building. I tried my husband's cell phone and couldn't get through.

I called my oldest sister, Arlene, and found that she had spoken to Valerie. She told me, "Don't worry, I know they left the office because I heard her over the phone." Valerie had been on the phone with Arlene, wishing her a happy birthday, just as the first tower was hit. Valerie threw off her headset and never hung up with Arlene. Arlene heard Valerie asking, "What was that?" and then heard a scream: "Everybody out, get out!" Arlene stayed on the phone for a few more minutes and heard silence; then the phone was cut off.

As I continued to answer phones, we started to receive calls from other Marriott Hotels, family members of coworkers, and media people trying to speak to anyone in the area. We heard an announcement to stay in our areas and not to vacate the building at this time. I didn't really know how bad it was getting outside. I realized later that by that time, the second tower had been hit, and the media was starting to call it terrorism.

Get Out of the Building!

My boss came in and said we should go ahead and vacate the building. I told him, "Just give me a minute because families are calling and everyone is concerned about their loved ones." He said, "Annette, we need to leave *now*, things are getting really bad, and I don't want any of you to be stuck in here—those buildings could go at any time." I wanted to stay there so I could hear that my sister was out of harm's way. I continued to try my sister's cell phone and my husband's to no avail. I got my mother and explained that I was all right and would contact her as soon as I knew what was happening. I could tell in her voice she was worried about my sister—she was still awaiting a phone call from her.

One of the last phone calls I took was from my wonderful neighbor, Evelyn O'Neil. I was surprised to hear her voice, and she was just as surprised to hear mine. She said, "Annie, you're still there?" and I said, "Oh Evelyn, it's crazy over here." She radioed her husband Brian, an NYPD officer, and said "Brian, she's still in her building." I told Evelyn, "Tell him not to worry, I'm just waiting to see if Valerie calls." Then I heard his voice clearly say, "Tell her not to worry about her sister and to get out of that building now!" That was when I realized I had to go!

I left the building with my boss Mike, my friend Barbara, and some other people. When we got outside, the sound of sirens filled the air, and debris was flying from the buildings. I saw body parts that our staff had covered with hotel linens. We heard a policeman directing people to go south and shouting, "Let's move it, people, we have another airplane coming!" Barbara and I looked at each other in shock. We headed south toward Battery Park, and when we reached the Brooklyn Battery Tunnel we found a few of our coworkers. Allison, the other pregnant woman, turned to me and said, "Annette, have you eaten anything?" It dawned on me that two hours had passed since my morning insulin shot and I had not eaten. Remarkably, Allison was still holding her egg sandwich. We decided to share it.

As we stood there in shock at the sight of those two towers burning, we saw people falling out of the building and more flying debris. No one was having any luck with their cell phones, except one girl who finally connected with her boyfriend. He told her about the plane that hit the Pentagon. At that news, everything began to feel unrealistic, like we were in a movie. As Allison and I were standing there eating our egg sandwich, we all of a sudden heard a roar.

It was the collapse of the first tower. We heard the rumble and saw the collapse, and I remember just sort of freezing in my spot. The girl on the cell phone literally pulled us and yelled, "We have to get out of here . . . RUN!" I threw my sandwich to the ground and yelled at Barbara to keep going, that I would catch up. I saw the cloud of soot and debris racing toward me and thought, *I am not going to be able to outrun this cloud, so I may as well slow down and avoid falling and hurting the baby.* I made my way to a black fence nearby, so I would have something to hold onto when the cloud hit. All of a sudden the cloud came right up on me and hit like nothing I have ever experienced before.

I wear a gold chain around my neck with a gold cross and charms with my children's birthstones. As I took in the smoke and tried covering my mouth with my shirt, I grabbed my chain and kissed the little Jesus. I said a quick "Our Father" and prayed, "God, protect my baby." I also prayed for my sister Valerie. I walked along the fence, trying to remain calm and taking shallow breaths. I remember thinking I would be okay, and this wasn't my time to die. I ran into Barbara and several coworkers, who immediately offered me water and told me to wash my mouth out. I could feel a burning sensation going down my throat and into my chest; my nostrils were filled with the smell of smoke.

We made it to Battery Park and sat on a bench to catch our breath. When the smoke cleared, I had a clear view of the Statue of Liberty. As I looked around, the complete horror of the situation hit me. Everyone started helping out; the vendors in the park were tearing open bottles of water and handing them out to everyone. We went to the American Café restaurant, and they were giving out water, wet towels, and napkins. We cleaned our eyes and wiped our faces. Then it started happening again—people started screaming, running, and trying to get out. The light fixtures started to tremble, and I knew it was the second tower falling.

We finally heard that the Staten Island Ferry was running. My friend Barbara convinced me to let her take me to her home in Staten Island, and to a hospital. On the ferry ride, I heard jets flying over and my boss said, "Don't worry, I'm sure they're ours." We went to Barbara's house, cleaned up, and called my OB doctor, who wanted me to get to a hospital immediately to be checked out. Once we got there they took in both Barbara and me immediately, did blood work, and checked our vitals. They hooked me up to a fetal monitor for about an hour. Everything checked out well with the baby and I was released. Barbara had an EKG done and she was also released.

I knew that with all of the bridges and tunnels closed there was no way I could get home that night. I wanted to see my family, but I was SO thankful to be there with Barbara. My sister Valerie had made it to Arlene's house in New Jersey, and my mother had taken my daughter there also. On Wednesday, I had three emotional reunions—first with my mother, then with my sister Valerie, then with my husband and children. I was so grateful and felt lucky that we were all alive, and that the baby was unharmed.

My mother, my daughter, and I went to church that evening. I felt emotionally drained, but as I entered the church and kneeled down to pray, I broke down in tears. I couldn't thank God enough for keeping the baby and my family safe. I prayed for all of those people who were lost as well as their families. I couldn't imagine how they must have felt or what they were going through . . . and I still can't.

I went on maternity leave a few weeks after 9-11. For the first month I was off, I was an emotional wreck. I couldn't stop crying, and I could not turn off the television. I almost became obsessed with it. My son did not want to talk about it (and he is still not comfortable with it, but he has dealt with it). My daughter has had the hardest time. She went through nightmares and became even more attached to me in the months following 9-11. My husband was and always is the strongest one in my family; he pretty much just let me deal with things in my own way. I guess he had to be strong enough for the both of us. He always has been my rock to lean on, and I love him very much for that.

After 9-11 I had to see the doctor on a weekly basis; I guess the baby helped keep my mind off of things and helped me focus on something other than this horrible thing that happened to our country. I was very concerned about the baby's health. When the baby was born in November, there were complications and he spent two weeks in the neo-natal intensive care unit. We delayed our Thanksgiving until he came home. We were so thankful to God for bringing him home safely. He has just turned one year old, and the strength this child exhibits has convinced me that he is going to grow up to be fearless. He has gone through MRIs, x-rays, evaluations, blood tests, and even wore a prosthetic helmet for a few months, and he *still* seems to be the happiest baby on earth. I guess maybe in some way he knows how lucky he is to be alive. I thank God every day that he is fine. I really believe God has put him here on earth for a reason.

I Still Trust God

I still view God in the exact same way as I did prior to 9-11. I still hold all my beliefs and trust in Him as I always have. I still strongly believe that everything happens for a reason, even though it may be hard to understand or explain why things are the way they are. I do attend church more often than I did in the past. I try harder to get my children to understand why it is so important. I hope to raise my children as good, strong Christians, and I pray to God every day to give my husband and me the strength and guidance to be successful parents to our children. I know He is still always there for me.

Still, not a day goes by that I don't think about 9-11. Sometimes it hits me and I think, *How could we have let this happen? How did it happen?* I still feel anger and at the same time fear about our future and the future of our children. I still worry about the safety of my family, and I wish that my other sister and my brother lived closer to me. I cherish my children even more than I did before (if that is possible). I try to make the most of our time, and I want them to learn to enjoy every minute of their lives. I want to teach them not to be afraid, and to make the most of their lives.

18

JUAN MEMBRENO

God Is My Provider

Juan Membreno is a gentle man who loves Jesus and
wants to serve Him. He has been a Christian for 16
years. He has always tried to be a minister in his jobs
and share God's love through the way he works. Before
the attacks on the World Trade Center, Juan was manager of stewards at the famous Windows on the World
Restaurant on top of the WTC. He loved his job.

On the morning of September 11, he was delayed in
getting to work for the first time in six years. As he was
getting ready for the day, he saw on the TV that the first
tower was on fire. He was worried for his coworkers and
tried to get in touch with them to no avail. Then he saw
the second plane hit, and a very short time later, both
towers collapsed. He was horrified, because he knew
that many of his coworkers were stuck on those top
floors and had most likely died. He was overcome with
guilt, as he knew he should have been there that day!

The first week after the attacks was hard for Juan.
The pain and sorrow in his heart was unbearable. Nightmares and guilt plagued him for quite a while. Not only

had he lost some very dear friends, he had lost his job. How would he cope, and how would he go on? The only thing that got him through this time was his relationship with Jesus Christ. He had trusted the Lord with many things in his past; he had to trust Him for this as well. He had no other choice and no other hope.

For months to come, the repercussions of September 11 continued. As Juan went from place to place to find income for his family, he struggled through the sea of red tape. One guy even told him that if he weren't so honest he would get through the process faster. Juan could not believe what he heard! He had done what he thought was right, and this is what he got! For many months he had no income, but Juan says that God came through with a check here and an envelope there to provide for his family. Through his own church and other Christians, Juan and his family found refuge and comfort. After months of waiting, Juan's old boss decided to open up a new restaurant; Juan was one of the former employees who were asked back to work. Juan has been able to minister to his coworkers who did survive—he prays for them and listens to them as they sort through their grief.

During the time that he was out of work, Juan's pastor encouraged him to do outreach through his fellowship, Thessalonica Christian Church. As he got busy, his own problems seemed small. He sees that God let him work with the homeless and others who were struggling to show him his own blessing. One blessing that he saw was that he and his family were all together and safe. Another was that God helped him get "out of himself" to help others even as he struggled himself.

As many people have said, this act of terror brought good to Juan. He came to a closer relationship with the

Lord and began new ways of ministering to others. He has found that God is developing in him a call to preach. One day when he was on the street, a woman yelled at him for preaching and was angry with him. The next day, she saw Juan again and he reached out to her in kindness. She was shocked that even after she yelled at him, he was nice to her. He got the chance to share with her why he was that way. The Lord can bring good things out of even very bad situations.

The thing that makes Juan happiest is to see people who have hit bottom in their lives come to know the Lord and get their lives right. Cleaning up on the outside can only last if the inside is clean too, according to Juan. He hopes to be able to bring the cleansing love of Christ to many people in the future.

Forgiving Osama

How is Juan coping? Well, he thinks every day about those who died. He believes that God is in charge and that He will bring justice in the end. One big hurdle he has had to overcome was forgiving Osama Bin Laden and his people. He feels that it is truly not a choice to not forgive him. The Lord calls believers to forgive out of obedience—not feeling. Juan feels free now, and that is what forgiveness is for, so that we can be free from hate and bitterness.

Juan wants to let people know that he is grateful for the prayers and concern that so many from all over the world have shown after the attacks. He has leaned on the Lord. Philippians 4:13 in the Bible has meant a lot to Juan as he has struggled through this time: "I can do everything through him who gives me strength." He is learning that each day is important. We don't know what we will wake up to each morning; we need to be prepared to face God one day. "We know our dates of birth, but we never know our dates of death," quotes Juan. He had told his coworkers, "See you tomorrow" when he left work on September 10. And he didn't see them anymore.

Juan hopes that he will have the chance to talk to people as they go through pain. He feels now that he has experienced pain so deep that it is inexpressible. He wants to tell them, "I'm passing through similar pain. The Lord is with you. You can feel peace. It's okay to cry and it's okay to be angry. God is big enough to handle your anger, even if it is directed to Him. The Lord gets me through this every day. He can get you through the burden that you carry."

As Juan shared his testimony, he beamed with joy as he mentioned all the things that God was doing and would do. Tears streamed down his face as he remembered his coworkers, some of whom may not have been Christian believers. Some he knew he would see again one day.

All along the way, Juan stayed on the right path. He could have lied and gotten money in an instant. He didn't. He could have thrown up his arms and walked away from God when the checks weren't rolling in, but he didn't. He trusted the One to whom he had committed his life. And once again, God was faithful in His promise that He would provide.

19

CHARLES AND ELLE OTT

Touched by a Mission Team

Charles and Elle Ott had lived in lower Manhattan for a long time. They are an older couple who have lived their lives to the fullest. Charles, who works for the city, and Elle, an art illustrator, lived in Gateway Apartments, one-and-half blocks from the World Trade Center. They enjoyed going for walks and sitting on the plaza at the WTC. Elle spent time there sketching, feeding the birds, and enjoying the crisp air that swept through the valleys created by the tall buildings around her. They found it a place of solace. Many times they enjoyed outside concerts there in the evenings. This was their community and it held many fond memories for them.

Elle had surgery just a few days before September 11 and was recovering in their home. When the first plane hit, Charles and Elle heard a boom and thought their own building had been hit at first. They tried to find out what had happened, but couldn't. The power in their building went out, so they had no idea what to do. When the towers collapsed, smoke and debris billowed all through the building and neighborhood. When they looked out the windows, all they saw was blackness. They feared the worst. Charlie was convinced that an atomic bomb had hit Manhattan.

Paralyzed with Fear

The couple found a radio that worked, and as they listened they were paralyzed with fear. Charlie was afraid of making Elle walk down the stairs, so they stayed put—for four days. Finally a national guardsman found them and, after much arguing concerning Elle's condition, escorted them out to a world that was different than they had known just days before. Through many twists and turns of finding a ride and getting out of the city, they went in search of a place to stay.

After some weeks of living in various locations, the Otts made it back to their apartment and found it full of soot. The management had hired some untrained workers to clean, but they had made it worse. Some neighbors had told them about a group of Baptist Christians who were cleaning apartments for free. They decided to take a chance. Not only did the workers clean their apartment exceptionally well, they showered Charles and Elle with a lot of love.

On the very first night back in their home, Charles and Elle woke to find that an electrical fire had set their couch ablaze. They got out and, although the damage was minimal, they didn't want to return. Too much had happened to them in those few weeks; they needed to start over somewhere else.

A friend recommended an apartment complex in the Bronx, far away from lower Manhattan, so Charles and Elle took the few belongings that they had left and moved. They were lonely, and the disaster was starting to catch up with them. They reached out to a local Baptist association office and asked for help. This association is a group of churches that combine their efforts in missions and ministry. Volunteers met with them, prayed with them, and started the ball rolling to get them some assistance.

When Beverly, a volunteer, came up to visit with them, she met two very distraught people. Charlie had been sober from alcohol for a long time, but had begun drinking again. Elle, who had chronic health problems, was severely traumatized by the whole event that had been playing out for almost two months. They couldn't even tell anyone exactly how much they were hurting, but those who visited them could see that it was taking a toll on their relationship and their health.

Over the next months, people continued to minister to them and walk through the valley with them. Both Charles and Elle had religious backgrounds but had never really committed to Christ. Several people talked with them and shared the gospel through being a support and loving them through the hard times. In fact, God used many different people to reach out to them. One time, Charles drank a lot of beer and hid the cans in the stove. While he was napping, Elle got home and turned on the stove to begin cooking dinner. After a few minutes, the stove was smoking so bad that they had to call the fire department. Little damage had been done, but the police officer that had arrived saw that it was neglect. He had a choice to take Charlie in. He pulled Charlie aside and told him that he was in recovery and that he needed to get to AA (Alcoholics Anonymous). If Charlie did that, he wouldn't arrest him. Charlie saw that as a wake-up call and an act of mercy from God. He went to AA and from that moment on stayed clean.

In March of 2002, a college mission team offered to clean Charles and Elle's apartment. Many of their possessions were still packed up and full of dust and soot. The girls on the team worked at the apartment several days in a row. Elle was very touched that these young women had spent their spring break helping her. As they sat and visited before they left, Elle asked them why they would do this. The girls told her clearly—it was because of their relationship with Jesus Christ. They asked her if she would like to invite Christ to live in her heart. She said yes and became a Christian that day. She prayed a beautiful prayer, asking God to help her to heal and to live in a way that was pleasing to Him. Charles continues to contemplate Christ, and he and Elle are healing slowly from the trauma of 9-11. Charles has found a great AA sponsor who is a Christian, and other believers have surrounded him and Elle and supported them along the way.

Charles and Elle can hardly believe all that has taken place. They know that the source of all good things is Jesus Christ. They have seen God work in their hearts, bringing healing and helping them feel settled in their new home. God is there, and they know that He will take care of them. God always seems to "show up" just when they need Him. They are growing in their trust of Jesus, with the help of brothers and sisters in Christ.

September 11 took a toll on Charles and Elle, but it didn't crush them. In Romans chapter eight, Paul reminds us all that no matter what comes our way, we cannot be separated from Christ. He says this: "Who shall separate us from the love of Christ? Shall trouble or hardship or persecution? . . . No, in all these things we are more than conquerors through him who loved us. For I am convinced that neither death nor life, neither angels nor demons, neither the present nor the future, nor any powers . . . will be able to separate us from the love of God that is in Christ Jesus our Lord" (Romans 8:35, 37–39).

20

INGRID ROBERTSON

"A Hand of Comfort Came Over Us"

What would it be like to run down 99 flights of stairs, praying all the way and not really knowing what had happened to you? That is what Ingrid Robertson of Brooklyn, New York, experienced on September 11.

It began as a typical day for her. Ingrid, a wife and mom of two children, caught the bus and subway into Manhattan that morning to her job at an insurance brokerage firm in Tower Two of the World Trade Center. Within minutes after she arrived, they heard that a plane had hit Tower One. Even though no announcement to evacuate was made, she and other coworkers decided to evacuate immediately. They began the long walk down. Ingrid took her shoes off and started down the stairs. After they had descended only a few floors, someone instructed them to go back to their offices. Something inside Ingrid told her to keep going. Minutes later, Tower Two shook. Ingrid knew something bad had happened. She decided to continue down the stairs.

When asked what was going through her mind, she says that she was thinking of her children, ages 15 and 4, and her husband back in Brooklyn. She froze for a moment and then began praying out loud. She noticed that others were praying out loud, asking Jesus to save them. All of a sudden, she says, "a hand of comfort came over us, and we felt a covering of God's Spirit, and we knew we would get out." She prayed for people along the way. She told her coworkers to rely on God because "He promised that He would never leave us or forsake us." About halfway down the stairwell, she immediately felt a peace come over her that went beyond her imagination. A voice inside told her to keep going down and keep praying for the other people. It was chaotic on every side, but she knew that God had arrived to bring help and reassurance.

When she got down to the bottom level, there was more chaos. She never looked back as she began a trek to Brooklyn. She couldn't find an available pay phone to call home, so as she walked she began to pray again. A cab showed up, and the driver said that the bridges and tunnels were all closed, so it would be hard to get to her home in Brooklyn. She asked him to take her to her sister's home in the Bronx. She got there in the early afternoon. That evening, she finally got in touch with her husband and children. They were all relieved. Ingrid stayed in the Bronx till the next day. She didn't sleep much that night. All night long she had dreams of the falling towers and not being able to escape.

She found out later that her boss had gone back to make sure everyone had gotten out, and he died. She knew then that the inner voice telling her to keep walking had helped her stay alive that day, because if she had gone back with her boss she would have been killed.

The days ahead were hard. She went to the doctor and was told that she had severe spinal and muscular injuries from running down the stairs. The trauma to her muscles was so bad that she couldn't walk for weeks. She was also in counseling for months dealing with the emotional trauma. At the time of this writing, she is still recovering but is back at work. She is trusting God for her transition back to work.

In October of 2001, through a coworker, Ingrid was able to get assistance for her family through a local Christian missions group. She was on disability but had not received any compensation because of all the chaos at her company. These Christians were able to help her for four months with basic bills, groceries, and Christmas toys for her two kids. Times were tough in the fall and winter because Ingrid had been the primary breadwinner in her family.

Ingrid spent most of her life in Brooklyn, New York. She met her husband at her job, and after dating for a while they got married and settled in as a young couple in love. A few years later she became pregnant with their first child, Kimberly, who is now 15. Kareem came along 4 years ago. Ingrid attended church growing up, but had never made a profession of faith until 1987, when Ingrid found God in an intimate way and began a new journey. She knew that she needed a personal commitment to the Lord in order to live life more fully. As she has grown in her faith, she has been given a keen sense of discernment. She prays and listens for those "nudges from God."

If you had met Ingrid before September 11, you would have seen her as a wife and mother who cared deeply for her family. She is a bright woman, faithful to her job. She was active in her church and teaches Sunday school. She was a good listener and an encourager to others. She did all the right things to be a "Christian." People liked her, and her children adored her. She lived her life in a comfortable manner until that day.

What is different now? She says she feels that God wanted her to wake up and see people in a different way. She has become more fervent in sharing her faith and ministering to people in very real ways, even while she was on her back recuperating. She has talked to others about what God has done as they came to visit her, and she challenged them about their own life and following God.

Ingrid also feels that God wants her to be more appreciative of people around her. Each day, her family spends more precious time together because of that urging from her experience. She sees now that every day could be the last day of her life, and she tries to live it fully. She continues to heal, and along with that she watches her children and husband heal. Her children are now fearful of her leaving the house, and as she gets better and gets out more, a whole new set of issues with her children are coming out. She assures them of her love, but most of all she teaches them about God's everlasting love, reminding them that God will never leave them or forsake them. She feels that this is a good learning experience for her children to see who God really is and what He can do. She makes it very clear that God can allow some to die and some to live, but with each situation, His purpose is to show His love and allow us to grow from the experience. They have seen their mom continue to praise the Lord even in her difficult situation. She shares her faith more fervently. She continues to encourage others, making sure that they get an extra helping of encouragement.

She feels that September 11 was a wakeup call for all Christians. Ingrid discerns that we have been somewhat lazy in telling the good news of Christ to others. She wants to tell Christians that we should be doing the work of the Lord in all areas of our lives, not just at church. She wants us to look around and see what God has brought to us to do and then do it. She hopes that we will all fervently pray for God's direction in our lives so that we can hear God when we need to. She was glad that she listened to Him in that stairwell on September 11.

Concerning trials and difficult times (including terrorist attacks), Ingrid feels that what she knew has been reinforced through this experience. She says, "When we put our hearts in the hands of God, fully believing and trusting in Him, then we can have peace and confidence, even when we are tried, tested, tempted, and tossed by the circumstances of life or troubled by the enemy. We will be refined like gold in the fire. Then we are ready for service of value. We become a useful tool in the hand of God to bring gladness, comfort, and joy to the hearts of many who are challenged by what life brings."

Ingrid smiles as she says again, "I tell you, I am so thankful that I am alive today! I will serve the Lord today and every day till I die! God doesn't have to tell me twice anymore."

21

DEL WILLARD

Fears Relieved

When you first meet Del Willard, you see a kind-faced gentleman in his sixties. His snowy white hair and twinkling blue eyes make it easy for people to respond to him as he greets them at East 7th Baptist Church on a Sunday morning, where his ministry is to help you to feel welcome. And welcome you he does! First you get a strong handshake or a big hug, and then he makes sure that you have a seat. If you are new, he will seat you with someone from the church so that you don't feel alone. One cannot feel like a stranger after meeting Del.

Del is one of thousands of actors in New York and has actually had the opportunity to act while in the city. He is originally from Rutland, Vermont, a place that is quite a contrast with New York City. Del goes to Vermont at least once a year, rekindles his spirit, and returns to the rigors of being an actor in the Big Apple. After September 11, though, Del was ready to go north and stay. Fear hit him, and in fact he did go to Vermont for about two months. At the time he went, he was ready to give it all up; he was fed up with the stress of the city and all the crazy things happening after the attacks. About mid-way into those two months, he realized that he was running, and it was about fear. During his stay in Vermont, he recognized that the attacks had opened up wounds from his family history and that to run from the city would not make them go away. Instead of giving in to his fears, he decided to go back to the city and face them.

When he got back in January of 2002, he delved into acting auditions like he never had before. He started a frenzy of busyness, like many of us do when we don't want to face something. Soon, he knew he had to get help. He was still feeling paranoid over the attacks and what the government was doing, and he didn't like what he was becoming. Doubt had come into his heart about everyone and their motives, and he knew that wasn't right. Something had to change.

Del is a Christian and a recovering alcoholic. He has been sober 32 years and credits his relationship with Jesus Christ, which he started in 1985, as the sole reason he has remained sober. September 11 rocked his world (like the rest of us), and even through that, he stayed sober. Many of his buddies who were in recovery did go back to drinking out of fear, but Del knew that his own strength would not get him through this; he needed the strength of Jesus Christ. And Jesus did help Del. After getting back to New York, Del asked a friend about Christian counseling services. He found a great counselor to help him walk through his fears and help him make sense of it all.

God is good! When we call on Him and ask his help, He comes to us with more than we can imagine. Del began a new phase of his relationship with Christ. What did Del learn from all of this that we can profit from?

First of all, Del found that he had some trust issues with God and with people. He wanted to feel safe, so he ran away to a place that seemed safe. When he got there, he realized that the fear of terrorism and distrust of people was still with him. It's not the place where we are, but the Person we place our trust in—Jesus Christ. Our government will fail us, our friends and family will fail us, but God will never fail us.

Second, Del has renewed his focus on whom he trusts. What he has found is that as he trusts God more and turns over his fear, he can look at people in a new light. He can see people for who they are: fragile, imperfect persons whom God loves and can redeem. Every person on this earth has value in Christ, and Del can help communicate that to others.

Del is not afraid of people anymore because his trust is in Christ. People are not the enemy. Osama Bin Laden is not the enemy. The government is not the enemy. It is the enemy Satan, who fosters evil. Del feels that we sometimes fear the person we think is our enemy. Evil is our enemy . . . not people! And Christ has overcome evil with good.

Del feels he has become complete in his faith. He recognized Jesus Christ as his Lord and Savior, and he knows his sobriety is a result of God's healing. But it has always been a challenge, because of his fears, to really reach out and meet people where they are. Del has rethought the command by Jesus to "love your neighbor as yourself" (Matthew 19:19). Feeling that he had been admonished, he saw Scripture and God communicating this message to him: "Del, don't say you love Me if you are not willing to love your neighbor." Del felt that he had a judging spirit of others. Until he saw his own humanity, he couldn't stop judging others' actions toward him. He feels free to love now and to let go of the things that bother him about others. He has what he needs now to really live for Christ. It's so simple, yet so hard when it is blocked by fear. To be free to love is the greatest gift that anyone can receive.

Del feels that God reinforced to him that community is good. We were not created to be "lone rangers." From the beginning of time, God created us for companionship. To say you don't need anyone is selfish, according to Del, because it goes against what God created us for. There is something false about having just a few select friends and excluding others. Del feels that the church can be that way sometimes without knowing it. We think that we can choose whom we should love, when in fact Scripture commands that we show love to all, regardless of who they are. We are to open ourselves up to all and love as Christ loved us . . . unconditionally. Del finds that since he has gotten out of himself and out of his fear, he is able to see others in a different light. He has been given a new heart, one that is free of fear, to love others more than he ever has. There is great satisfaction in letting your heart be healed. You are free! No more baggage! No more torment!

Del is not unlike many people in New York City. He didn't know anyone personally in the towers. His job wasn't affected. He lived far enough away that he didn't see the soot and debris near him. Crisis counselors say that September 11 affected far more than those in the buildings and their families. The despicable act of terror brought up past fears and hurts that people may have experienced earlier in life. If someone had a trauma as a young person, some aspect of it would probably be brought back up by the terrorist attack. A lot of people have walked around with fear and paranoia and other symptoms of post-trauma disorder without realizing it. They think any trauma was only for those directly related to the towers.

A lot of old family hurts came up for Del on the day of the attacks. He attributes the process of healing to God's love and care for him. He encourages others to seek help if past hurts have come up or you just don't feel like yourself. Trauma can spark the revival of feelings from even 20–30 years ago! God is our healer, and He promises us that we will be healed one day. Del looks forward to that day of completion when he sees Jesus face to face. His favorite quote now is one from Franklin D. Roosevelt: "The only thing we have to fear is fear itself." Del understands what that means now!

22

STEPHANIE WONG

Leaning Not on Her Own Understanding

Stephanie Wong, 23, is the middle child of three children in the Wong family from Queens. On September 11, 2001, she and her sister Jennifer headed into Manhattan to go to work. Stephanie works for a Wall Street firm, JP Morgan Chase, a few blocks from the World Trade Center. Her sister Jennifer worked at World Trade Center One. They had done their usual morning routine that day, walking around to different stores window-shopping and then going their separate ways. As they parted, Jennifer asked Stephanie, "Where are you going?" Stephanie thought that was a bit odd, but she just thought, "That's Jennifer." Those were the last words that Stephanie would hear from her sister.

Stephanie reached her office building and was getting coffee when the building shook. The security guard yelled, "Oh my God . . . Look!!" She looked outside and saw papers flying everywhere. Rumors started circulating that a helicopter had hit the WTC, so she went to her office and called home. When she spoke to her mom, they realized that the tower that had been hit was the one where Jennifer worked. Stephanie tried several times to call her sister, but the phones were out. Cell phones weren't working that day either. She could receive calls but couldn't call out. Friends called, and Stephanie began hearing that Jennifer's office might have been hit.

The second plane hit the second tower and, once again, Stephanie's building felt the shock. She and her coworkers decided to get to safety on the ground floor. Not knowing what to think, she prayed for her sister as she made her way down the stairs. As they got out to the sidewalk, a huge black cloud of dirt and smoke came after them. They ran down the street and ran into a drug store that was open. The dust and debris went past them.

They were given water and towels at the drugstore. Stephanie suggested that some coworkers walk toward Chinatown with her. They got to Stephanie's church, where they washed and cleaned up. Her friends went home, but Stephanie waited to hear some word on her sister and another member of the church who worked at the WTC. Her family and some church friends started a massive search of every hospital and every nook and cranny of lower Manhattan.

By the end of the day, they knew that Jennifer had died. A person from Jennifer's company explained to the family that Jennifer's desk was only feet away from where the first plane entered the building. She had most likely died quickly.

Stephanie and her family knew that Jennifer was a Christian and was now home with her Father, but that did not take away the pain and loss they felt. Stephanie says that her faith walk was crazy that first year after losing Jennifer; she continues to have up and down days. She went through the gamut of emotions. Stephanie and her family are grateful that they all have faith in the Lord and that Jennifer is with Jesus. That brings comfort.

Stephanie has seen God work in the last year. Old friendships have been rekindled. A friend came to know the Lord this past year because of the way Stephanie and her family handled their grief. Many people who were "on the fence" concerning their faith have been drawn back to the Lord. Stephanie also has found a renewed relationship with her Lord.

When asked what she thinks about what happened to her sister and others, Stephanie is quick to say that there are no easy answers. She does know that God did not "do this" to us. She knows that God is faithful and though we may not understand all that has happened, we can trust Him. There is also the hope that in tragedy, good can come. Nothing that happens is surprising to God. He is in control.

There are two specific Scriptures that have been helpful to Stephanie. One is Psalm 46:10, which says, "Be still, and know that I am God." This verse has caused Stephanie to stop when things get crazy and focus on what is important. Another is Proverbs 3:5–6, which says, "Trust in the Lord with all your heart and lean not on your own understanding; in all your ways acknowledge him, and he will make your paths straight." Stephanie truly believes that God will guide her even on turbulent days. God is there, and Stephanie will keep walking even in the midst of sorrow.

Read the story of Stephanie's sister, Jennifer Wong, also included in this book.

23

DAVID DEAN

Thoughts on 9-11-01

D r. David Dean is the former director of missions of the Metropolitan New York Baptist Association and a poet. He expresses his grief and sorrow and faith through his poetry. Below are some of his writings since 9-11.

Clouds
9-13-01

There's a hole in the New York skyline
And a vacuum in our hearts
As we struggle hard with disbelief
And wonder where to start
To heal our broken spirits
With love from heart to heart.

Clouds of smoke still hover
Where once proud towers stood
While clouds of grief engulf us
As we search for the good.

This cloud upon our city
Is more than we can bear
Unless we walk together
To show how much we care.

Two Brothers
(After a trip to Ground Zero 9-18-01)

I met two brothers
Yesterday
Resting
Just a few yards from the pit of hell
That contained the remains of
Thousands of victims
Including
Their own brother.

Pain was etched on the
Faces of firemen
Policemen
And rescue workers
Emerging from the rubble
Where smoke still rose from the hell below.

How Are You Doing?
10-11-01

"How are you doing?" so many have asked.
"Terrible!" I reply, and it is the truth.
How can we be otherwise with so many who
Have died and such horror persists?

How have we made it this far?
How shall we carry on?
We are borne on the prayers of believers
Who share our burden of grief.
A deep haze encloses the city still
And lonely, the Empire stands
While deep in the pit, fire smolders.
"When, O Lord, will this end?"

Hope

12-20-01

"And now abideth faith, hope, and love . . ."
The brackets of hope are two of life's greatest virtues,
The object of our faith is the Lord Jesus,
The driving force of our faith is love,
Hope is the glue that holds them together.

How long we held out hope
For victims of September's sad disaster.
Firefighters dug in the rubble
Hoping to find just
One of their brothers alive.

Hundreds of families
Searched the streets and hospitals
Hoping to find
Their loved ones clinging to life.
Parents waited patiently
Hoping their children would come home
That terrible Tuesday.

"If in this life we only have hope."
The misery of death engulfs us and we will
Drown in our sorrow and self-pity.
Because of Christmas, and the
Obedient Son of God,
Who gave His life for our sins,
We have HOPE now and forever!

Hope is . . .
The anchor for the soul
Awash in awesome waves of grief.

Hope is . . .
The steel that sustains our faith
Under direct attack from the enemy.

Hope is . . .
The assurance that Incarnate Love
Has already won the ultimate victory!

AND NOW . . . MY STORY

24

LISA CHILSON-ROSE

God Loves New York

I woke up on September 11, 2001, in a city that I had come to love passionately over the last 17 years. It was a clear, beautiful day. Fall was setting in, and it was going to be full of things to do. I was thinking of my wedding, which was less than 2 weeks away, and rejoicing at the great meeting the association had the night before.

I loved Tuesdays, staff meeting day for those of us who worked at the Metropolitan New York Baptist Association. We spent a lot of time praying in staff meeting, and that always left me energized for the day. As I was getting ready, my coworker, Michael Chance, called and said that something had happened at the World Trade Center. I turned on the TV and every channel was covering it. They were speculating that a small plane had accidentally crashed into the towers. That seemed odd to me, but in New York nothing is a surprise!

I live at the Baptist Building in Manhattan, so as people started coming into work, they came to the apartment and gathered around the TV, watching in awe. Then I saw it. A plane was coming toward the towers—it sailed right into the South Tower and exploded. We were stunned. At that moment I realized this was no accident. My fiancé, Russ, called from his parents' home about 25 miles away to check on me. I wanted him here with me, and if we had known that the city would soon be in a lockdown, he would have come down immediately. Unfortunately, we were apart for days.

My coworkers and I started praying. Our hearts were heavy, and everyone was starting to feel the pain, knowing how many people were in the towers. I will never forget what happened moments before the first tower collapsed. On one of the local stations, anchors had gotten a cell phone call from a young guy who was stuck in his office on one of the upper floors of Tower One. He was telling the anchor where he and others were. "I'm in the southwest corner of the 86th floor. I'm under a desk and I think there are a few others here with me." He kept repeating that. The tone in his voice was begging for someone to find him. He couldn't get out of his office. Within minutes after they hung up, the towers collapsed, one by one. We were in shock. That guy's voice kept haunting me for days; he couldn't have gotten out.

We saw that a plane had also hit the Pentagon in Washington, D.C., and one had gone down in a field in Pennsylvania, and we were really worried then! Being missionaries and ministers, the staff all wondered what we should do that day. We checked the phones and saw that the lines were dead. A couple of us went to the roof and tried our cell phones to no avail. Of course there were no lines! All of our cell phone towers had been on top of the trade center. No phones, no cells, no Internet. TV lines were down. I had cable, and that was the only way we knew what was happening downtown. Everyone was in shock. We didn't know what would happen next. We were all desperately trying to strategize, wondering about our families in other places, trying to get in touch with them. I was sad because by this time I realized Russ would not be able to get down here. Every means of transport was shut down into New York City. Deep breath . . . along with other staff, we began to strategize.

We had heard that people were walking uptown because all public transportation was shut down. We also knew that they would be walking our way, as the office is right on a main thoroughfare of Manhattan's Upper West Side. So we pulled out tables and got cold water ready to give to passersby.

As people began to creep uptown, they were covered with dust and debris and were in a state of shock. We opened our chapel, and staff was on standby to minister to those who stopped. We got a chance to talk to quite a few people that day. Their stories were incredible—they had experienced such horror. I was amazed that such chaos was going on only four miles south, because initially it was so peaceful and normal in our neighborhood.

We continued to minister to those weary travelers all day and into the evening. Some staff stayed over at the association's building because they couldn't get home that night. I remember lying across my bed, exhausted. After I drifted off to sleep, I woke in a panic as the sight of the towers collapsing and that guy crying out for help on the television ran through my dreams. I didn't sleep well that night as I grieved over what had happened. There were many nights over the next year and a half when that image and others would creep into my dreams, and panic would overcome my peaceful sleep.

Although I am originally from Birmingham, Alabama, I consider myself a New Yorker after being here so long. As a New Yorker, you come to think that nothing could happen to you, that you could endure anything. That mindset catches on as you live here. You feel invincible. But on September 11, all New Yorkers were reminded how fragile life really is and how quickly it can be snuffed out. We were humbled that day to our knees.

The association team continued outreach for months following the attacks. As Baptists sent disaster teams in to work, the days were long and exhausting for everyone. Visits to fire stations and police stations began. I tell people that on September 11, 2001, we started a workday that wasn't really over until the end of 2002. For almost a year, volunteers came and supported the disaster work here, and Christians from all over the world reached out to us. Our office became a clearinghouse for donations of cards of encouragement, teddy bears, food, Bibles, gloves, and other items to give out at Ground Zero and surrounding areas. Bags of perfume and lotions, and books on grief crowded the volunteer's office for quite a long time. I have been a missionary for more than 17 years, and I was still amazed at how God's people acted in this devastating time, reaching out and loving New Yorkers.

On September 22, 2001, I became a married woman at the age of 40. Two weeks before, I was wondering if we were going to be able to have a wedding. Family members and friends were wondering if it was safe to fly, drive, or come to New York at all. I was frantic. I couldn't believe I had waited this long to get married and a terrorist attack was going to ruin it.

I had many thoughts about marriage, commitment, and tragedy over the course of those two weeks. God was so gracious to sustain me through it all. I realized that someone I loved could be killed or die in a minute, and I would lose a precious person. It made me glad that both Russ and I were committed to the Lord and that we knew this earthly life was just one part of our journey with Him.

So many emotions flooded my thoughts those weeks. I thought about all the brides-to-be on the news who had lost a fiancé and were devastated, some whose weddings were to be the same day as ours. I was hurting because I felt like our wedding had been contaminated by such an evil act. I was grateful because so many people reached out to Russ and me to help us get through those last two weeks.

September 22, 2001, was another gorgeous day. I woke up that morning feeling a peace that I couldn't imagine feeling on a wedding day. Many people were praying for us that day, and it was obvious! As I went through the preparations of getting ready, many people commented that I was "too peaceful," and I told them that it was God's peace. Our families and most of our friends had made it, and by the time the ceremony started, the room was packed with over 140 guests. We had a beautiful time and everything went perfectly. We decided to add to the ceremony a time of remembrance for our city, and it was touching. Our hearts joined together to lift up the city to God, the only One who could bring comfort to our hurting hearts.

As we left the ceremony, we went out on the front steps of Metro Baptist Church, and as cars came by, they honked with joy for us! We all needed a day celebrating the goodness of life. We needed that day of enjoyment. That evening, there was a big New York kind of dinner, celebrating with our friends and family, saying, "Look what God has done!"

Life over the past couple of years has been challenging, tiring, and astounding. To see God sustain our new marriage when so much chaos was going on around us, to see Him begin to heal a city and unify Christians to share God's love in such tangible ways was astonishing. I have been through some trying times and God has always increased my faith during those times, but He has been more real to me than ever during the years since 9-11. To see God work in healing me and others the way He has is marvelous.

A few days after the attacks, I went with some friends from North Carolina to the makeshift memorial at Union Square Park, a mile from Ground Zero. We were watching people and looking at all the posters and notes and candles. I did a double take when I saw a simple sheet of white paper that said:

I ♥ NEW YORK
—God

Scribbled below was Psalm 46:1–2a: "God is our refuge and strength, an ever-present help in trouble. Therefore we will not fear." I suddenly felt safe, and I remembered Who was really in charge of this world.

One Scripture that comes to mind often in the years since 9-11 is Isaiah 30:20–21— "Although the Lord gives you the bread of adversity and the water of affliction, your teachers will be hidden no more; with your own eyes you will see them. Whether you turn to the right or to the left, your ears will hear a voice behind you, saying, 'This is the way; walk in it.'" We have learned to listen to God's voice more than ever before, and He has guided us. To God be the glory for the great things He has done!